FRENCH

AT

HOME

Way Usable French for Families

Written by Adelaide Olguin

created with love by
TALKBOX.MOM
Talk in a foreign language with your family!

To the greatest language teachers in the world—
mothers.

YOUR HOME IS A
POWERFUL PLACE.

IT'S WHERE YOU
LEARNED YOUR
FIRST LANGUAGE.

IT'S WHERE YOU
TAUGHT YOUR CHILD
THEIR FIRST LANGUAGE.

AND IT'S WHERE,
YOUR FAMILY
CAN LEARN THEIR
SECOND OR THIRD.

OPENING CREDITS

Thank you to the incredible women who ensured you'll talk like they do with their families in their native language and not like you walked out of a dusty, old textbook.

Joanne Rouzic de Souza   Elissa Mleiel
Valérie Renard   Armelle Bevilis
Justine Baer   Charline Leroi

The French in this book was developed with a focus on the French spoken at home in France, more specifically in the region of Paris.

Previous high school students should note that in spoken French "on" is used instead of "nous" and inverted questions are not used. We also did not use any outdated, textbook words. Instead, we used words and expressions that families are actually using.

Some words may vary from region to region or across different French-speaking countries. We tried not to use region-specific words so that you can converse well in France, as well as other French-speaking countries.

Do note that it is common for French speakers to describe a word to another French speaker from a different region to communicate words that are region-specific.

If you find yourself in another country (which I do hope you do!), you can start adding region specific words to your sentences. Then you'll know two ways to say things and be even more impressive.

Table of Contents

There is native speaker audio for every single phrase in this book, plus a system to help you track your progress as you listen, practice, and use your phrases in the **TalkBox.Mom Companion App.**

At the time of your purchase, you received non-transferable app access directly tied to your email address. If you don't already have access to the audio from the time of your purchase, please email your receipt to support@talkbox.mom so we can get you set up in the app.

To download the TalkBox.Mom Companion App on your phone, search for "TalkBox.Mom Companion App" inside your phone's app store (Android or Apple). After downloading the app, log in with your username and password. You can reset your password using your email address on the login page if you have no idea what your password is.

If you have any other problems or questions, please email support. Our team would love to help you!

♥ support@talkbox.mom

Hello! Of Course.

Many people think that learning a language starts with colors, numbers, and the ABCs. But that's what our kids do in preschool after they can already speak the language.

This is not where language learning begins. And starting with the ABCs and colors is definitely not language immersion or the path to fluency.

There is hardly another civilised nation so dull in acquiring foreign tongues as we English of the present time; but, probably, **the fault lies rather in the way we set about the study** than in any natural incapacity for languages."
- Charlotte Mason[1]

Learning to use a language looks like starting your day off, greeting each other, and eating in that language. It looks like grocery shopping in that language while helping each other or sometimes hearing kids complain. If your extended family speaks that language, it looks like using that language at family events. If your family doesn't, it looks like telling your child to go back, flush the toilet, and wash their hands in your "secret language." ;) Everyone else will be impressed by your language skills—not knowing how gross your child is being.

At TalkBox.Mom, we help families, like yours, start talking in a foreign language the exact same day they start. You don't wait to talk until year two or year... well, never. You talk from day one.

We can help your family start talking right away because we copy the approach of the best language teachers in the world: parents.

Yes, parents. Think about it. Who taught your kids to talk before they ever learned grammar and reading? You did.

As moms and dads, we teach babies and toddlers all over the world to talk at a native level—the most coveted level of learning a language. We have a higher success rate of teaching languages than high schools, colleges, and universities.

With TalkBox.Mom, we give you the tools to learn and teach another language using our proven roadmap and various fluency approaches based on natural language progression. We also help you lean into the skills you already have to teach a language successfully as a parent.

Plus, everything in our language programs are made by native-speaking women who want you to sound like you're from their country—not like you walked out of an outdated textbook.

And, yes, there is audio for every single phrase in our program. We mean it when we say that we'll give you all the tools to make learning another language feel easy, fun, doable, and the biggest confidence boost you've ever gotten.

And now, with your family, you get to use a language with this phrasebook and hear it for yourself!

My Story

Before I read the words of Charlotte Mason and M. Gouin, I too realized that "the classical method, with its grammar, its dictionary, and its translations, is a delusion."[2]

You see, my husband and I put everything in storage to travel around the world with our two boys to play and explore outside. We started in Brazil, and I had a verb conjugation book, a college textbook, vocabulary cards, and two little boys to learn Portuguese with!

I had tried learning other languages this same way (well, minus the little boys)—only to leave me feeling anxious whenever I went to speak. But this is how learning a language is done, right? 😣

When I announced to my three-year-old that we needed to learn to conjugate a verb before going outside, he stared at me like I was out of my mind and said, "We didn't come to Brazil to sit in a room."

And I realized that he said this wise statement without ever learning to conjugate verbs or without ever looking at flashcards. As someone who studied philosophy and languages at the University, I was self-aware enough to realize that I had been sucked into a very flawed but widespread model of language learning. It hit me that parents teach languages so much faster and before their kids can read—without grammar and vocab worksheets.

So I decided that I was going to teach a language like a mom and learn like a child with my family. Within two weeks, I was shocked when we were talking in and understanding Portuguese with native speakers in Brazil. Absolutely shocked. And as the months rolled on, we kept talking and understanding more and more.

From country to country, I continued to develop and optimize this approach as we traveled for two years. Each time we learned faster and were reaching our goal: really speaking the language! Queue a whole ton of fireworks!

But this wasn't enough. I knew any family could learn a language this way. Not just mine. I could feel it in my heart. You specifically were in my heart. Your hopes, your dreams of being able to use another language with your family. Before I ever met you here, I was thinking about you and knew I needed to do this for you.

So I created TalkBox.Mom with an amazing team of women to give you life-changing results.

I know that when you and your family can actually use a language, you can change your future work and educational opportunities. You can help others in your community. You can connect with family. You can make real connections as you travel. You can truly become a global citizen.

If you don't have your first box to use with this phrasebook, go to **www.talkbox.mom/french**! Then please introduce yourself in our private accountability group. You'll get a private invitation exclusively for families in our signature program: The TalkBox.Mom Boxes.

I'd love to know what led you to want to learn a language with your family and which language you chose.

I want to meet you! I want to hear your progress and see you reach your daily goals. After all, I made TalkBox.Mom for you.

See you there!

xo

Adelaide Olguin

How to Guide

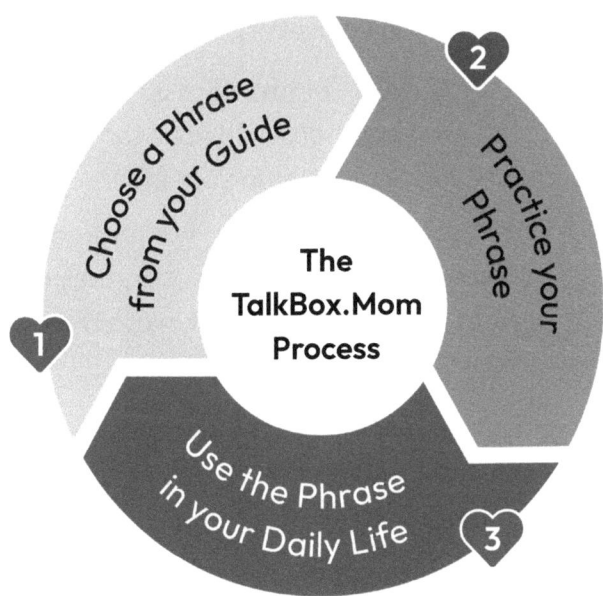

The TalkBox.Mom Process

1. Choose a Phrase from your Guide
2. Practice your Phrase
3. Use the Phrase in your Daily Life

The TalkBox.Mom Process has three completely doable steps to get your family talking

First, you pick your 1-5 Focus Phrases. Yes, full phrases—not individual words or verb conjugations.

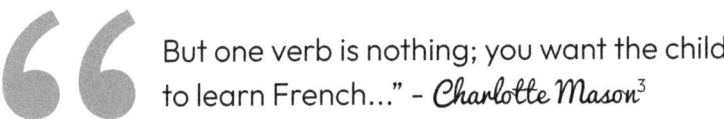

But one verb is nothing; you want the child to learn French..." - *Charlotte Mason*[3]

We recommend picking the bulk of your phrases from the boxes and one phrase every couple of days from the phrasebook or other guides like the Homeschool Phrases.

Second, you'll practice the phrases. It's very important to practice your phrases so your children are ready to use them in real life, which brings us to our next step!

Third, you'll use those phrases in real life. The goal is to add the phrases to your everyday life!

By following the TalkBox.Mom Process, you'll be learning to use full sentences with your family and continue to use those phrases in your life.

 Of course, his teacher, will take care… that as he learns new words, they are put into sentences and kept in use from day to day." - *Charlotte Mason*[4]

Here's a closer look at how these steps will look in your day with your family as well as some things to avoid!

Step 1: Pick 1-5 Focus Phrases

🕐 Time Needed: typically 30 seconds to 2 minutes

The first step is to choose only one to five Focus Phrases. This step is actually really hard for many people because it's so tempting to want to start with, well, everything! However, I promise that you'll learn everything much faster if you focus on one to five phrases.

Why? By focusing on a small number of phrases, you'll learn those phrases faster and deeper than if you spread yourself too thin. You'll also be able to give the phrases the attention they need to be practiced and used in real life. It's much more doable to implement two phrases with your child than 20 in a single day.

 That they should learn a few—two or three, four or five—new French words daily...." - *Charlotte Mason*[5]

Even if it feels "too light" for you as the parent, the goal isn't that you're learning a whole bunch of things. It's that you're using the language. Using the language requires a deep and narrow focus that consistently grows.

This small focus helps lay a strong foundation. As these phrases are really internalized when they are practiced and used, they start to feel like second nature (aka a second language).

When this happens, the following sets of phrases you work on continue to become even easier, especially if you start your first box in the TalkBox.Mom program because it's designed to help you make exponential progress.

So please allow yourself to learn everything faster by focusing on one to five phrases—not by focusing on everything all at once.

> To start, have your child color in the heart of one phrase in this guide.

I recommend starting with just one phrase your first day so you can take the phrases through the entire

TalkBox.Mom Process.

If you have the first box, start with the first phrase on your Challenge Checklist, and then in your second practice session add one phrase from this phrasebook.

As you work through this phrasebook, pick Focus Phrases that:

#1. You NEED to say.
#2. You WANT to say.
#3. You say ALL THE TIME.

Do not start at the beginning of this book by learning phrases from A-Z. You'll make faster progress if you focus on choosing phrases that have your family's specific needs and wants—not by learning every phrase. That's because languages are built on needs and wants—not grammar and vocabulary.

Well before grammar school, we use language to get what we need or want. This is the reason children start talking. If screaming, crying, and making obnoxious sounds don't work, they will use language to get that cookie or ball or to help us see something they LOVE.

To start, look for phrases that grab your attention. For example, if you get in the car often and need everyone to buckle up, section "Car" under chapter C would be a great place to start.

If your siblings are constantly bothering you, "Don't"

under chapter D is a great place to start. If you love to play with bubbles, "Bubbles" under chapter B would be a great place to start.

First, go through and mark your highest priorities, and learn those first. Then move on to secondary things.

Next, you just need to be a rebel. Don't pick Focus Phrases that aren't applicable to your family. Like, if you aren't changing diapers in your home or you don't tell your child, "No," skip those phrases. No need to email me with your parenting philosophy. I trust you to make the best choices for your family.

With that said, if you can add the phrase to your life—even if you don't say it in English, by all means, learn that phrase so that you can add it to your life and practice speaking French.

Also, feel free to change phrases you wouldn't use by replacing them with other nouns you would use. For example, you might switch the word "baby bag" to "backpack." If you're using our boxes with this phrasebook, you'll find so many opportunities to mix and match a ton of phrases.

You can always go back to learn anything you skipped later. Maybe another baby will come into the picture. ☺

When you choose the Focus Phrase for your Phrase Practice Session, you can choose the phrase in front of your child, you can give your child two good options and allow them to choose the one that they're more excited about today, or you can let your child choose.

Have you or your child heart the phrase in the TalkBox.Mom Companion App for easy access to the audio and progress tracking.

Open your TalkBox.Mom Companion App included with your purchase or verified gifting of this book (see page 9 for instructions). Click on the book icon ▣ on the home screen. Then select Use French at Home. After selecting the letter of the alphabet that coordinates with the section in which your phrase appears, slide the top section and click the bolded title that appears above or with your phrase.

Next, have you or your child click the heart ♥ next to the chosen phrases. Now your phrases will easily be accessed from the home screen under "Practicing." This will help save you time in the next steps!

For families with multiple children, you can alternate who hearts phrases or have your other children help in the following steps. If your child does not look at screens, they can listen to the audio without viewing your phone.

Step 2: Practice your Phrases
🕐 Time Needed: 2 minutes to 10 minutes

Note: The more phrases you've chosen, the longer this step will take.

For older children with required foreign language time of 30, 45, or 60 minutes a day, this step can expand to that time requirement, keeping in mind that Step 3 will give you additional time, especially as you're able to use more of the language.

The second step is to practice your chosen phrases. There are three main ways to practice your phrases, and they're listed here in order of importance: (1) practice with the native speaker audio, (2) practice in situations, and (3) practice with emotions.

❶ Practicing with the Native Speaker Audio

" That children should learn French orally, by listening to and repeating French words and phrases."- *Charlotte Mason*[6]

You might be tempted to skip this step if you, as the parent, can pronounce the phrases or if you're a native speaker, but don't skip it! It's important to have that extra input that's not just you. Get that extra input! There's a noticeable difference if you skip practicing with the native speaker audio.

To practice with the native speaker audio, navigate to your practicing section or the book in the TalkBox.Mom Companion App as described in the previous step. Be sure "autoplay" is turned off in the app because you want to practice one phrase at a time—not repeat all your phrases together.

Have you or your child announce what the phrase is in English and tell everyone to repeat after the native speaker. For example, "We're going to hear how to say, 'Buckle up,' in French. Have fun repeating after each word. If you can, say the full phrase after her at the end."

The native speaker will say the phrase word by word while pausing for your family to repeat. Then she will say the full phrase and pause for your family to repeat.

If the full phrase feels like too much at first, that's fine! Just say the phrase word by word. After a couple of days, you'll feel ready to say the entire phrase.

After you finish repeating the phrase, have you or your child ask everyone what the phrase means. If some family members aren't sure, remind your family what it means, practice with the audio again, and ask again what the phrase means until everyone is on the same page.

When your family repeats with the audio, celebrate that everyone tried! Refrain from correcting anyone's pronunciation or being hard on yourself for how you sound.

Why? For family members over four years old, it can take a couple of weeks to a couple of months to hear the sounds in the new language, and when you can't hear the sounds, you can't fix the sounds. So if you tell someone they're saying it wrong, and they can't hear it to fix it, they'll just be annoyed with you.

But you can start hearing better as you're having fun as you listen and practice with the native speaker audio. The keyword here is fun! Stressed-out people have trouble hearing better. So be sure not to stress your kids or yourself out by focusing on sounding perfect.

Focus on having fun so you can continue to hear the sounds over time and improve as you continue to practice and use your phrases.

② Practice the Phrase in Situations

Once your family repeats with the native speaker audio, practice that same phrase in a situation rather than moving on to the next phrase. You can absolutely play the audio again and again as you practice the phrase together.

To make this phrase real for your family and make your practice age-appropriate, decide together when you could add this phrase to your life. You can either set up that specific situation and practice using the phrase in that situation, use the phrase as you pretend you're in that situation, or say the phrase like you're in that situation. Yes, details to follow.

For example, if the phrase is, "Follow the path," you could walk over to a path with your family and have one family member say the phrase and another family member follow the path. Then switch until everyone has had a turn to say the phrase!

Or you could pretend there is a path in your living room and have one family member say the phrase and another family member follow the path. Then switch until everyone has had a turn!

Or you could sit on the couch or ground outside (because it's just one of those days) and have a family member say the phrase like they see a path and want someone to follow it.

You can raise the stakes in any of these situations and say, "Say, 'Follow the path,' like you're on a secret mission in the jungle." Or, "Say, 'Follow the path,' like it leads to ice cream!" We call this game, "Say It Like." Let the creativity spill over here. Younger and older kids will have different ideas that match what's fun and interesting for their age level.

❸ Practice your Phrase with Emotions

Here's where you can have even more fun! This is an extra important step if you've ever corrected your child's pronunciation, making them shut down or be less willing to try. And it's equally important if this has ever happened to you, and you have hesitations about speaking another language. Remember, it's more important to have fun than to sound perfect.

To practice with emotions, we have three outlets. The first is choosing raw emotions and having someone say a phrase with that emotion.

For example, "Say the phrase, 'Follow the path," like you're really happy!"

You can choose any emotion or state, like excited, sleepy, scared, nervous, creepy, or hangry.

The second way to practice emotions is by saying the phrase like you're someone else. Choose a person your child knows. This could be a friend, superhero, or character. For example, "Say the phrase, 'Follow the path," like Grandma."

The third way to practice a phrase with emotions is with music! Different styles of music can make you feel different ways. You could sing your phrase like an opera singer or rap artist. Whatever musical style you or your child likes or wants to try. And you don't have to be on tune to make this jam session effective.

After you practice your phrase, go back to Part 1 and listen to your next phrase repeating these two steps.

Q: What should I do if my child is an infant or toddler?

A: Practice and use your phrases around your infant or toddler! He or she doesn't need to repeat with the audio or practice saying the phrases yet to learn. This is a great age for them to take in what you're doing and learn from you.

Step 3: Use your Phrases

At this point, "lesson time" is over, and real life begins!

It only be a little lesson, ten minutes long, and the slight break and the effort of attention will give the greater zest to the pleasure and leisure to follow."
- *Charlotte Mason*[7]

> Now it's time to encourage everyone to try to add your phrases to your day as many times as you can before your next Phrase Practice Session!

Celebrate any attempt at using phrases. Even if only a word or two come out!

If you forget to use a phrase and remember it moments later, use it right then! Start building that habit.

And please! Don't deprive yourself of looking at the phrase or listening to the audio again to help you say that phrase. You might feel like you're cheating or like you need to force yourself to remember. Nope. Make it very easy for yourself until it feels like second nature. If it doesn't feel like second nature, you need to look and listen again to continue to build that neural pathway.

Now, if someone in your family uses one of your phrases and another family member forgets what the phrase means, tell them what it means! You want to make it easy for your children to know what's going on. They just put in all the work to learn their first language, which now feels super easy to them. If the second language feels difficult, there can be more resistance.

So say the phrase in English if someone is confused and then again in the language that you're learning. We call this the "Ice Cream Sandwich" because you first say the phrase in the other language, then in English to clarify, and then in the other language again.

As you use your phrases as a family, our goal is fun—not perfection. The fastest way to improve is to elevate the journey—not the finish line.

If you have a family member who already speaks French and is constantly correcting or just sometimes corrects you... or you want to make sure you are on the same page, ask him or her to read the love letter on the next page.

Dear smart and clever French speaker of the beautiful person who came over to you, asking you to read this,

     I know it's really hard, so please try your best to avoid nitpicking at how your family pronounces and says things in French, and also please refrain from correcting every little thing. I know you want to help, and, as you might know, constant correction will not actually help your loved ones to learn. It will silently break their hearts, make them angry with you, and make them want to quit.

Instead, continue to talk to your family in French and answer their questions. It will help them so much. Over time, in their time, they will learn from your example as well as from their Practice Sessions with this phrasebook. Plus, you will score major points for being nice, positive, and patient. Yes, of course, you're welcome.

Your Daily Schedule

The daily French lesson is one that should not be omitted." - *Charlotte Mason*[8]

As your next Practice Session starts in two hours or the next day—depending on the speed you want to progress—check off the phrase(s) from your previous Practice Session to indicate that you practiced the phrase(s).

Record your previous Focus Phrases from the phrasebook in sets of 10 phrases max. Before each Practice Session, quickly review a set of previous Focus Phrases by either practicing the phrase with an emotion or in a situation as you play the audio. It should take 10 - 15 seconds to review each phrase.

Then complete your next Practice Session, and work together as a family to use the phrase(s) as much as you can.

Remember, to quickly hear a Focus Phrase again and again, click "Practicing" on the home screen of the app where your hearted phrase is saved.

"

I was a French major in college, and I've learned more functional French in the last two months with TalkBox.Mom than I ever learned in all that time!

- Heidi Greening -

Our family is having such fun speaking to each other and challenging each other. I didn't expect the family-building, family-strengthening benefits that would come from this.

- Kathryn Winterscheidt -

TalkBox.Mom works great for a mix of older and younger kids learning together. We're all enjoying learning and using French!

- Elizabeth Huang -

Not only has the program inspired and instructed us in French, but the TalkBox.Mom approach to pedagogy has taught me how to be the teacher and the mother I dream of being.

- Isabella Leake -

You're Invited!

TalkBox.Mom boxes, our signature program, are excellent to use along with your phrasebook because you'll make more progress using them together—without adding any extra strain to your day.

Each box has a different fluency approach than the phrasebook. For example, the fluency approach of the first box, the Snacks and Kitchen Box, is consistency and exponential progress.

To create consistency, we not only link speaking French to a specific activity you do daily, but we also link it to a specific area in your home. To help you make exponential progress, the patterns that we chose for your family lay a strong foundation of the language and open you up to being able to say more than just the phrases you're focusing on.

And like I said, you'll spend the same amount of time practicing phrases. Your Practice Sessions will still have 1-5 Focus Phrases. However, you'll pick the bulk of your phrases from your boxes.

In the phrasebook, you skip topic to topic rather quickly. However, each box focuses on a specific topic and each Challenge narrows that focus to create a full sequence. With these sequences, you learn phrases faster and go deeper.

With that said, the phrasebook has such varied phrases that this keeps foreign language exciting and allows you to add more varied phrases to your life. This is the perfect complement to the patterns you find in the boxes. For this reason, you'll find that you'll use the phrasebook throughout all nine of the boxes.

As you use the phrasebook with the boxes, you'll start hearing your family use French throughout your entire day.

How do the boxes work?

Each box has three Challenges with a different language guide for each Challenge. The language guide might be a sequence of phrases, a poster mixing and matching full phrases, label cards with full phrases to use common items in your home, or an activity to do with your family.

You'll spend one week to one month per Challenge. During that time, your goal is to complete at least 10 Phrase Practice Sessions. If you're competitive and complete more Practice Sessions during that time, then awesome!

After at least 10 Phrase Practice Sessions, you move on to your next Challenge in the box. You don't learn every phrase in your Challenge. Rather, you start with high-priority phrases and work your way down. And when you come back to a Challenge later, because you've been using your phrases, you learn the rest of the phrases even faster. Yes, faster than if you tried to learn every single phrase before moving on.

After you complete at least 10 Phrase Practice Sessions for each Challenge, move on to your next box!

Boxes can be delivered once a month, every two months, or every three months. It's also possible to pick your own delivery dates or pause based on your needs—like if you're going to France to use your French, you can have a couple of boxes delivered together to take with you and choose a date further out for your next box.

With each box, you facilitate a high-level immersion experience that would cost at least $750 each time you work through a box <u>per person</u>. We put that experience into a $90 box for your family. And if you love to save money, you can pre-purchase all your boxes and save.

So if you'd like to go even deeper in French and have more fun with us, I'd love to invite you to purchase your first box or all nine.

Go to **www.talkbox.mom/french** and checkout with the same email address you purchased the book so that all your programs are together!

After that, you'll be invited to an exclusive bonus for our signature program: our Accountability Community. Here you'll be able to share your progress as you work through your Challenges, get ideas for your Practice Sessions in the boxes, and connect with other families who are learning to use French together!

I can't wait to see you there!

What The Banner?

WHAT ARE THESE LITTLE BANNERS THROUGHOUT THE BOOK?

These banners let you know where we go deeper into these topics in the TalkBox.Mom signature program.

The phrasebook can be used on its own or—for an elevated experience—it can be used with the boxes.

The second is my favorite because you're able to use the language more consistently and make exponential progress due to the various fluency approaches used in the boxes. Plus, with the phrasebook, you're able to add phrases from different topics, mixing and matching phrases from the phrasebook with the grammar patterns you've mastered with phrases in the boxes.

I've sprinkled these banners throughout the book so you can see where we go deeper in the signature program and decide if you're ready to take the plunge of a lifetime.

Go to **www.talkbox.mom/french** to join us!

Add French

phrases

to your

daily life.

More details on page 17.

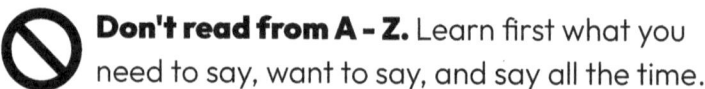
Don't read from A - Z. Learn first what you
need to say, want to say, and say all the time.

Native speaker audio for every phrase!
Go to: www.talkbox.mom/use-french-audio/

You'll find notes next to some phrases.
Find out how to use *(to 2+)* or *(to a mixed group)*.

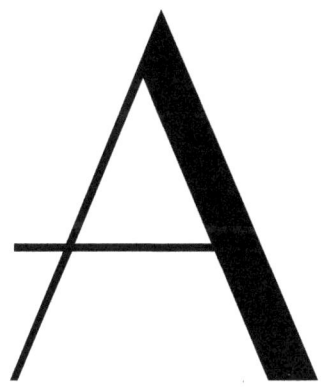

learn it!

♥ ☑ *Got it!*

♡ ☐ **Again!** **Encore !**

♡ ☐ Try again. Réessaie.

♡ ☐ *(to 2 or more children)* Réessayez.

♡ ☐ Do you want to play again? Tu veux rejouer ?

♡ ☐ *(to 2+)* Vous voulez rejouer ?

♡ ☐ Let's play again. Viens, on rejoue.

♡ ☐ *(to 2+)* Venez, on rejoue.

♡ ☐ I want to watch the video again. *(Can we play the video again?)* On peut remettre la vidéo ?

A

♥☑

♡☐ I need to change your diaper again. — Je dois encore changer ta couche.

♡☐ Please wash your hands again. — Lave-toi encore les mains, s'il te plaît.

♡☐ (to 2+) — Lavez-vous encore les mains, s'il vous plaît.

♡☐ **All done!** **Fini !**

♡☐ **Finished!** **Terminé !**

♡☐ I'm all done. — J'ai fini.

♡☐ Are you all done eating? — Tu as fini de manger ?

♡☐ Are you all done taking a bath? — Tu as fini de prendre ton bain ?

♡☐ I can tell that you are all done. — Je vois que tu as fini.

GET LANGUAGE GUIDES FOR SNACKS, DRINKS, MEALS, AND DINING IN THE TALKBOX.MOM SUBSCRIPTION

A

❤️☑️

🤍☐ **All gone!** **Il n'y en a plus !**
(*no more of it*)

🤍☐ The water is all gone. Il n'y a plus d'eau.

🤍☐ The chips are all gone. Il n'y a plus de chips.

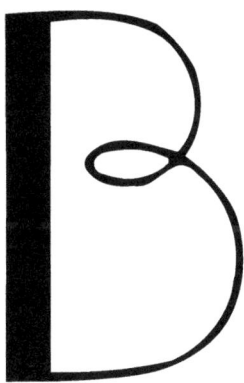

♥☑ *Got it!*

the baby bag	**le sac à langer**
I need to pack the baby bag.	Je dois préparer le sac à langer.
Did you pull everything out of the baby bag?	Tu as tout sorti du sac à langer ?
(to 2+)	Vous avez tout sorti du sac à langer ?
Where is the baby bag?	Où est le sac à langer ?
I can't find the baby bag.	Je ne trouve pas le sac à langer.

B

♥☑

♡☐ Can you please help me look for the baby bag? | Tu peux m'aider à chercher le sac à langer, s'il te plaît ?

♡☐ *(to 2+)* | Vous pouvez m'aider à chercher le sac à langer, s'il vous plaît ?

♡☐ Help me find the baby bag, please. | Aide-moi à chercher le sac à langer, s'il te plaît.

♡☐ *(to 2+)* | Aidez-moi à chercher le sac à langer, s'il te plaît.

♡☐ It's in the baby bag. *(masculine item)* | Il est dans le sac à langer.

♡☐ *(feminine item)* | Elle est dans le sac à langer.

♡☐ Are the wipes in the baby bag? | Les lingettes sont dans le sac à langer ?

♡☐ I think so. | Je crois.

B

♥ ☑

♡ ☐ **the babysitter** **la baby-sitter**
(*about a female*)

♡ ☐ (*about a male*) **le baby-sitter**

♡ ☐ ...is babysitting ... vient ce soir.
tonight. (*is coming
tonight*)

♡ ☐ The babysitter is La baby-sitter est là.
here. (*about a female*)

♡ ☐ (*about a male*) Le baby-sitter est là.

♡ ☐ Are you available to Tu es disponible pour
babysit on Friday garder (*name*) vendredi
night at seven soir, à partir de
o'clock? (*for one child*) dix-neuf heures ?

♡ ☐ (*for 2+ children*) Tu es disponible pour
garder les enfants
vendredi soir, à partir
de dix-neuf heures ?

the backyard **le jardin**

♡ ☐ Do you want to play Tu veux jouer dans le
in the backyard? jardin ?

B

♥☑

♡☐ Let's play in the backyard. | Viens, on va jouer dans le jardin.

♡☐ (to 2+) | Venez, on va jouer dans le jardin.

♡☐ The kids are in the backyard. | Les enfants sont dans le jardin.

♡☐ I left my (toy) car in the backyard. | J'ai laissé ma (petite) voiture dans le jardin.

♡☐ I left my doll in the backyard. | J'ai laissé ma poupée dans le jardin.

♡☐ Did you leave your bike in the backyard? | Tu as laissé ton vélo dans le jardin ?

♡☐ Go put it away. (the bike) | Va le ranger.

♡☐ (the toy car) | Va la ranger.

TALKBOX.MOM

B

❤️ ☑️

bad (*naughty or evil*) **mal**

(*not good*) **pas bien**

(*dull*) **mauvais**

♡ ☐ I did something bad. J'ai fait une bêtise.

♡ ☐ That was bad. Ce n'était pas bien.

♡ ☐ (*a movie*) C'était mauvais.

♡ ☐ Don't swear. That's bad. Ne dis pas de gros mots. C'est mal.

the ball **la balle**

(*inflated only*) **le ballon**

♡ ☐ Let's play with the ball. Viens, on joue à la balle. / au ballon.

♡ ☐ (*to 2+*) Venez, on joue à la balle. / au ballon.

♡ ☐ Do you want to play with the ball? Tu veux jouer à la balle ?

♡ ☐ (*to 2+*) Vous voulez jouer à la balle ?

♡ ☐ Take the ball. Prends la balle.

♡ ☐ Give me the ball. Donne-moi la balle.

B

❤ ☑

♡ ☐	Roll the ball.	Fais rouler la balle.
♡ ☐	I got it.	Je l'ai attrapée.
♡ ☐	You got it.	Tu l'as attrapée.
♡ ☐	Put the ball down.	Pose la balle.
♡ ☐	Pick up the ball.	Ramasse la balle.
♡ ☐	Throw the ball.	Lance la balle.
♡ ☐	Catch the ball.	Attrape la balle.
♡ ☐	You caught the ball!	Tu as attrapé la balle !
♡ ☐	I missed the ball!	J'ai raté la balle !
♡ ☐	I caught the ball!	J'ai attrapé la balle !
♡ ☐	Good catch!	Bien rattrapé !
♡ ☐	Nice throw!	Beau lancer !
♡ ☐	Get the ball.	Va chercher la balle.
♡ ☐	(to 2+)	Allez chercher la balle.
♡ ☐	Kick the ball.	Tape dans la balle.
♡ ☐	The ball went under the couch.	La balle a roulé sous le canapé.
♡ ☐	Don't throw the ball in the house.	Ne joue pas à la balle dans la maison.

B

❤️ ☑️

♡ ☐   *(to 2+)*   Ne jouez pas à la balle dans la maison.

♡ ☐   Play with your ball outside.   Va jouer dehors avec la balle.

♡ ☐   *(to 2+)*   Allez jouer dehors avec la balle.

the balloon	**le ballon (de baudruche)**
Look at the balloons!	Regarde les ballons !
I am blowing up balloons.	Je suis en train de gonfler les ballons.
Help me blow up the balloons.	Aide-moi à gonfler les ballons.
Don't put the balloon in your mouth.	Ne mets pas le ballon dans ta bouche.
I'm sorry. You cannot have a balloon. *(for a male)*	Je suis désolé. Tu ne peux pas avoir de ballon.
(for a female)	Je suis désolée. Tu ne peux pas avoir de ballon.

B

♥☑

the Band-Aid®	**le pansement**
♡☐ Do you want a Band-Aid®?	Tu veux un pansement ?
♡☐ I need a Band-Aid®!	Il me faut un pansement !
♡☐ Leave your Band-Aid® on. *(Don't take your Band-Aid® off.)*	N'enlève pas ton pansement.

the basket	**le panier**
♡☐ Put your toys in the basket.	Mets tes jouets dans le panier.
♡☐ *(to 2+)*	Mettez vos jouets dans le panier.
♡☐ The basket is empty.	Le panier est vide.
♡☐ Don't stand on the basket.	Ne te mets pas debout sur le panier.
♡☐ You're breaking it.	Tu es en train de le casser.

B

♥ ☑

the bath	**le bain**
♡ ☐ It's bath time.	C'est l'heure du bain.
♡ ☐ Did you take a bath already?	Tu as déjà pris ton bain ?
♡ ☐ You need to take a bath.	Tu dois prendre un bain.
♡ ☐ *(to 2+)*	Vous devez prendre un bain.
♡ ☐ It's your turn to give the kids a bath.	C'est à ton tour de donner le bain aux enfants.
♡ ☐ It's your turn to give him/her a bath.	C'est à ton tour de lui donner le bain.

> BATHING WALL CHART, HYGIENE GUIDES & BATHROOM LABEL CARDS IN THE TALKBOX.MOM SUBSCRIPTION

the batteries	**les piles**
♡ ☐ The toy needs batteries.	Il faut mettre des piles dans le jouet.
♡ ☐ The batteries are dead.	Les piles sont mortes.

B

♥☑

♡☐ I need to put new batteries in your toy. — Je dois mettre des piles neuves dans ton jouet.

♡☐ I put new batteries in your toy. — J'ai mis des piles neuves dans ton jouet.

♡☐ We need to buy some batteries. — Il faut qu'on achète des piles.

♡☐ Do not put the battery in your mouth. — Ne mets pas les piles dans ta bouche.

♡☐ We do not play with batteries. — On ne joue pas avec les piles.

the bed — le lit

♡☐ You need to make your bed. — Il faut que tu fasses ton lit.

♡☐ (*to* 2+) — Il faut que vous fassiez votre lit.

♡☐ Don't jump on the bed. — Ne saute pas sur le lit.

♡☐ (*to* 2+) — Ne sautez pas sur le lit.

♡☐ Don't eat food in your bed. — Ne mange pas dans ton lit.

B

♥ ☑

♡ ☐   (*to* 2+)   Ne mangez pas dans votre lit.

♡ ☐   Did you wet the bed?   Tu as fait pipi au lit ?

♡ ☐   **Bed time!**   **Au lit !**

♡ ☐   (*to toddlers and children*)   **Au dodo !**

♡ ☐   It's time for bed.   C'est l'heure d'aller au lit.

♡ ☐   Get in your bed, please.   Va dans ton lit, s'il te plaît.

♡ ☐   (*to* 2+)   Allez dans votre lit, s'il vous plaît.

♡ ☐   Please tell me a story before bed. (*Will you tell me a story before sleeping, please?*)   Tu me racontes une histoire avant de dormir, s'il te plaît ?

♡ ☐   Please tell us a story before bed. (*Will you tell us a story before sleeping, please?*)   Tu nous racontes une histoire avant de dormir, s'il te plaît ?

B

♥ ☑

♡ ☐   Good night!   Bonne nuit !

♡ ☐   I love you.   Je t'aime.

♡ ☐   (to 2+)   Je vous aime.

♡ ☐   Stay in your bed.   Reste dans ton lit.

♡ ☐   (to 2+)   Restez dans votre lit.

♡ ☐   Don't get out of your bed.   Ne sors pas de ton lit.

♡ ☐   (to 2+)   Ne sortez pas de votre lit.

♡ ☐   Stop playing, and lie down please.   Arrête de jouer et couche-toi, s'il te plaît.

♡ ☐   (to 2+)   Arrêtez de jouer et couchez-vous, s'il vous plaît.

♡ ☐   Go back in your bed.   Retourne dans ton lit.

♡ ☐   (to 2+)   Retournez dans votre lit.

♡ ☐   Go back to your room.   Retourne dans ta chambre.

♡ ☐   (to 2+)   Retournez dans votre chambre.

♡ ☐   Go back to your rooms.   Retournez dans vos chambres.

♥☑

♡☐ You can't fall asleep if you are not lying down. — Tu ne pourras pas t'endormir si tu ne te couches pas.

♡☐ (to 2+) — Vous ne pourrez pas vous endormir si vous ne vous couchez pas.

♡☐ Please go to sleep. — Dors, s'il te plaît.

♡☐ (to a toddler) — Fais dodo maintenant.

♡☐ (to 2+) — Dormez, s'il vous plaît.

♡☐ (to 2+ toddlers) — Faites dodo maintenant.

♡☐ The kids are finally asleep. — Les enfants se sont enfin endormis.

♡☐ The baby is finally asleep. — Le bébé s'est enfin endormi.

the bib   le bavoir

♡☐ Here's your bib. — Tiens, ton bavoir.

♡☐ Do you want your bib off? — Tu veux enlever ton bavoir ?

♡☐ You need to keep your bib on. — Tu dois garder ton bavoir.

♥ ☑

the Bible | **la Bible**

♡ ☐ It's time to read the Bible. | C'est l'heure de lire la Bible.

♡ ☐ Come sit down. We're reading the Bible together. | Viens t'asseoir. On va lire la Bible ensemble.

♡ ☐ *(to 2+)* | Venez vous asseoir. On va lire la Bible ensemble.

big *(masc. / fem.)* | **gros / grosse**

(masc. / fem.) (also) | **grand / grande**

♡ ☐ Do you want the big car or the little car? | Tu veux la grosse ou la petite voiture ?

♡ ☐ I'm a big boy. | Je suis un grand garçon.

♡ ☐ I'm a big girl. | Je suis une grande fille.

the bike | **le vélo**

♡ ☐ Do you want to ride your bike? | Tu veux faire du vélo ?

♥ ☑		
♡ ☐	*(to 2+)*	Vous voulez faire du vélo ?
♡ ☐	I want to ride my bike.	Je veux faire du vélo.
♡ ☐	Let's ride our bikes.	Viens, on va faire du vélo.
♡ ☐	*(to 2+)*	Venez, on va faire du vélo.
♡ ☐	Where is your bike?	Où est ton vélo ?
♡ ☐	Outside.	Dehors.
♡ ☐	In the yard.	Dans le jardin.
♡ ☐	In the garage.	Dans le garage.
♡ ☐	Please put your bike away.	Range ton vélo, s'il te plaît.

the binky   la tétine

♡ ☐	Where is the binky?	Où est la tétine ?
♡ ☐	I can't find the binky.	Je ne trouve pas la tétine.
♡ ☐	It's missing.	Elle a disparu.

B

♥ ☑
♡ ☐   Here's your binky.   Tiens, ta tétine.

to bite   mordre

♡ ☐   Take a bite of your sandwich.   Croque dans ton sandwich.

♡ ☐   Three more bites.   Encore trois morceaux.

♡ ☐   Don't bite me.   Ne me mords pas.

♡ ☐   *(to 2+)*   Ne me mordez pas.

♡ ☐   Don't bite your sister.   Ne mords pas ta soeur.

♡ ☐   Don't bite your brother.   Ne mords pas ton frère.

♡ ☐   Don't bite her.   Ne la mords pas.

♡ ☐   Don't bite him.   Ne le mords pas.

♡ ☐   No biting.   On ne mord pas.

♡ ☐   She bit me! *(for a male)*   Elle m'a mordu !

♡ ☐   *(for a female)*   Elle m'a mordue !

♡ ☐   He bit me! *(for a male)*   Il m'a mordu !

♡ ☐   *(for a female)*   Il m'a mordue !

B

☑

| **the blanket** | **la couverture** |
| **the blanky** | **le doudou** |

♡ Here is your blanket. Tiens, ta couverture.

♡ Where did you put your blanket? Où tu as mis ta couverture ?

♡ I can't sleep without my blanket. Je ne peux pas dormir sans ma couverture.

♡ I found your blanket. J'ai trouvé ta couverture.

♡ Don't drag your blanket on the ground. Ne laisse pas ta couverture traîner par terre.

♡ **Bless you!**
(after someone sneezes) **A tes souhaits !**

the blocks **les cubes**

♡ Let's play with your blocks. Viens, on joue avec tes cubes.

B

♥ ☑

♡ ☐   *(to 2+)*   Venez, on joue avec vos cubes.

♡ ☐   Let's make a giant tower.   Viens, on construit une tour géante.

♡ ☐   *(to 2+)*   Venez, on construit une tour géante.

♡ ☐   Please hand me a block.   Passe-moi un cube, s'il te plaît.

♡ ☐   Wow! You made a huge tower.   Waouh ! Tu as construit une énorme tour !

♡ ☐   *(to 2 +)*   Waouh ! Vous avez construit une énorme tour !

♡ ☐   Don't knock over my tower.   Ne casse pas ma tour.

♡ ☐   *(to 2+)*   Ne cassez pas ma tour.

♡ ☐   He knocked over my tower.   Il a cassé ma tour.

♡ ☐   She knocked over my tower.   Elle a cassé ma tour.

♡ ☐   Let's knock over the tower.   Viens, on casse la tour.

♡ ☐   *(to 2+)*   Venez, on casse la tour.

♥☑

♡☐   Please put your blocks away.   Range tes cubes, s'il te plaît.

♡☐   (*to* 2+)   Rangez vos cubes, s'il vous plaît.

the blood   le sang

♡☐   I'm bleeding.   Je saigne.

♡☐   He is bleeding a lot.   Il saigne beaucoup.

♡☐   She is bleeding a lot.   Elle saigne beaucoup.

♡☐   He bled a little bit.   Il a saigné un petit peu.

♡☐   She bled a little bit.   Elle a saigné un petit peu.

♡☐   Don't touch the blood.   Ne touche pas le sang.

♡☐   My nose is bleeding.   Je saigne du nez.

Blow!   Souffle !

♡☐   Blow on your food.   Souffle sur ta nourriture.

B

♥ ☑

♡ ☐   *(to 2+)*   Soufflez sur votre nourriture.

♡ ☐   It's hot.   C'est chaud.

♡ ☐   Blow out your candles!   Souffle tes bougies !

♡ ☐   Don't blow out your brother's candles.   Ne souffle pas les bougies de ton frère.

♡ ☐   Don't blow out your sister's candles.   Ne souffle pas les bougies de ta soeur.

♡ ☐   Blow your nose with a tissue. *(Blow your nose.)*   Mouche-toi.

the boat *(a toy)*   **le bateau**

♡ ☐   Here is your boat.   Tiens, ton bateau.

♡ ☐   You can take your boat in the bathtub.   Tu peux prendre ton bateau dans ton bain.

the boogers   **les crottes de nez**

♡ ☐   You have a booger.   Tu as une crotte de nez.

B

❤☑

♡☐   Don't pick your nose.   Ne mets pas les doigts dans ton nez.

♡☐   Blow your nose.   Mouche-toi.

♡☐   Grab a tissue.   Prends un mouchoir.

♡☐   Don't wipe your boogers on your shirt.   N'essuie pas tes crottes de nez sur ta chemise.

♡☐   Don't flick your boogers.   Ne lance pas tes crottes de nez.

♡☐   Don't eat your boogers.   Ne mange pas tes crottes de nez.

the book   **le livre**

♡☐   Let's read together.   Viens, on va lire ensemble.

♡☐   *(to 2+)*   Venez, on va lire ensemble.

♡☐   Which book do you want to read?   Quel livre tu veux lire ?

♡☐   *(to 2+)*   Quel livre vous voulez lire ?

♡☐   Did you like the book?   Tu as aimé le livre ?

♥ ☑

(*to* 2+)   Vous avez aimé le livre ?

I liked the book.   J'ai bien aimé le livre.

the bottle   **le biberon**

I need to give the baby a bottle.   Il faut que je donne le biberon au bébé.

Would you please give the baby a bottle?   Tu veux bien donner le biberon au bébé, s'il te plaît ?

It's time for your bottle.   C'est l'heure du biberon.

GET A LANGUAGE GUIDE FOR BREASTFEEDING & BOTTLES IN THE TALKBOX.MOM SUBSCRIPTION

the large toy box   **la grande boîte à jouets**

the small toy box   **la petite boîte à jouets**

Please put your toys in the box.   Mets tes jouets dans la boîte, s'il te plaît.

B

♥ ☑

♡ ☐   Are you hiding in the box?   Tu te caches dans la boîte ?

♡ ☐   Take the lid off the box.   Enlève le couvercle de la boîte.

♡ ☐   Put the lid on the box.   Mets le couvercle de la boîte.

♡ ☐   Open the box.   Ouvre la boîte.

♡ ☐   Close the box.   Ferme la boîte.

♡ ☐   Let me open the box.   C'est moi qui ouvre la boîte.

♡ ☐   Let me close the box.   C'est moi qui ferme la boîte.

♡ ☐   Your ball is in the box.   Ta balle est dans la boîte.

to break   **casser**

♡ ☐   What did I just hear break?   Qu'est-ce que je viens d'entendre se casser ?

♡ ☐   Who broke the vase?   Qui a cassé le vase ?

♡ ☐   Who broke the window?   Qui a cassé la fenêtre ?

B

♥☑

♡☐ Who broke the toy?   Qui a cassé le jouet ?

♡☐ Who broke the plate?   Qui a cassé l'assiette ?

♡☐ I broke the plate.   J'ai cassé l'assiette.

♡☐ The chair broke.   La chaise s'est cassée.

♡☐ The toy is broken.   Le jouet est cassé.

to take a break   faire une pause

♡☐ Let's take a break.   On fait une pause ?

♡☐ You need to take a little break.   Tu as besoin d'une petite pause.

GET A LANGUAGE GUIDE FOR BREASTFEEDING &
BOTTLES IN THE TALKBOX.MOM SUBSCRIPTION

---

to breastfeed   allaiter

♡☐ I need to nurse the baby.   Il faut que j'allaite le bébé.

B

♥ ☑

♡ ☐   I need to nurse the baby in fifteen minutes.   Il faut que j'allaite le bébé dans quinze minutes.

♡ ☐   I need to nurse the baby in one hour.   Il faut que j'allaite le bébé dans une heure.

♡ ☐   I need to nurse the baby in two hours.   Il faut que j'allaite le bébé dans deux heures.

the broom   **le balai**

♡ ☐   I need to sweep the floor.   Il faut que je passe le balai.

♡ ☐   Please hand me the broom.   Passe-moi le balai, s'il te plaît.

♡ ☐   Where is the dustpan?   Où est la pelle ?

♡ ☐   Sweep the trash into the dustpan.   Ramasse les saletés avec la pelle.

♡ ☐   Put the trash into the trash can.   Mets les ordures à la poubelle.

♡ ☐   I already swept the floor.   J'ai déjà balayé le sol.

♡ ☐   Don't make a mess.   Ne mets pas le bazar.

B

♥☑

♡☐   (*to* 2+)   Ne mettez pas le bazar.

♡☐   I just swept the floor!   Je viens de passer le balai !

to brush   **brosser / se brosser**

♡☐   Let's brush your hair.   Viens, on va te brosser les cheveux.

♡☐   (*to* 2+)   Venez, on va vous brosser les cheveux.

♡☐   Please brush your hair.   Brosse-toi les cheveux, s'il te plaît.

STEP BY STEP LANGUAGE GUIDE FOR BRUSHING TEETH
WITH CHILDREN IN THE TALKBOX.MOM SUBSCRIPTION

---

to brush teeth   **se laver les dents**

(*also*)   **se brosser les dents**

♡☐   Let's brush your teeth.   On va te laver / brosser les dents.

♥ ☑
♡ ☐   Please brush your teeth.   Lave-toi / Brosse-toi les dents, s'il te plaît.

the bubbles   les bulles

♡ ☐   Let's play with bubbles.   Viens, on fait des bulles.

♡ ☐   *(to 2+)*   Venez, on fait des bulles.

♡ ☐   Pop the bubbles!   Eclate les bulles !

♡ ☐   Blow some more bubbles.   Fais encore des bulles.

♡ ☐   Do you want me to blow some bubbles?   Tu veux que je fasse des bulles ?

♡ ☐   *(to 2+)*   Vous voulez que je fasse des bulles ?

♡ ☐   Don't blow so hard.   Ne souffle pas si fort.

♡ ☐   Blow soft, and it will work.   Souffle doucement et ça va marcher.

♡ ☐   Dip the wand in again.   Trempe encore la baguette.

♡ ☐   Put the wand in the bubbles.   Trempe la baguette dans le produit.

B

♥☑
♡☐   Close the lid.   Ferme le bouchon.

the bucket   le seau

♡☐   Put the rocks in the   Mets les cailloux dans le
        bucket.   seau.

♡☐   Let's fill the bucket   On va remplir le seau
        up with water.   avec de l'eau.

♡☐   Fill your bucket with   Remplis ton seau avec
        sand, and then flip it   du sable et renverse-le.
        over.

♡☐   Pull the bucket   Mets le seau bien droit.
        straight up.

♡☐   You made a sand   Tu as fait un château de
        castle!   sable !

to burp   roter

♡☐   I need to burp you.   Il faut que tu fasses ton
        (*You need to burp.*) (*to a*   rot.
        baby)

♡☐   Did I burp you   Tu as déjà fait ton rot ?
        already?

B

♥☑

♡☐ Hey. Don't burp in my face. (*to a child*)   Eh, ne me rote pas à la figure.

♡☐ Stop burping.   Arrête de roter.

the bus   **le bus**

♡☐ We need to go to the bus stop.   Il faut qu'on aille à l'arrêt de bus.

♡☐ The bus is coming.   Le bus arrive.

♡☐ Get on the bus.   Monte dans le bus.

♡☐ (*to 2+*)   Montez dans le bus.

♡☐ Get off the bus.   Descends du bus.

♡☐ (*to 2+*)   Descendez du bus.

♡☐ **Bye!**   **Au revoir !**

♡☐ Good to see you!   Ça m'a fait plaisir de te voir !

♡☐ (*to 2+*)   Ça m'a fait plaisir de vous voir !

♡☐ See you tomorrow!   À demain !

B

♥ ☑

♡ ☐ See you later!   À plus tard !

♡ ☐ See you soon!   À bientôt !

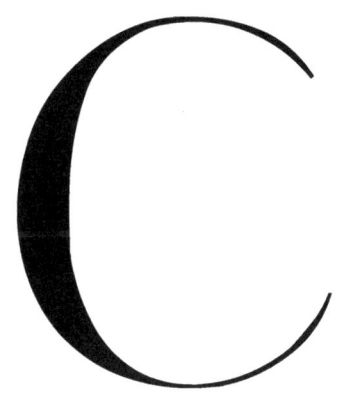

C

learn it!

♥ ☑ *Got it!*

♡ ☐   **Calm down.**   **Calme-toi.**

♡ ☐   *(to 2+)*   **Calmez-vous.**

                              the camera   **l'appareil photo**

♡ ☐   Let's take a picture.   Viens, on prend une photo.

♡ ☐   *(to 2+)*   Venez, on prend une photo.

♡ ☐   *(more guiding)*   Allez, on prend une photo.

C

♥☑

♡☐ Look at the camera! Regarde l'appareil !

♡☐ (to 2+) Regardez l'appareil !

♡☐ Looks great! Elle est super !
(the picture)

♡☐ Let's take one more. On en prend encore une.

the car   la voiture

♡☐ Go to the car. Va à la voiture.

♡☐ (to 2+) Allez à la voiture

♡☐ Get in the car. Monte dans la voiture.

♡☐ (to 2+) Montez dans la voiture.

♡☐ Get in your seat. Assieds-toi dans ton siège.

♡☐ Get in your car seat. Assieds-toi dans le siège-auto.

♡☐ Get in your seats. Asseyez-vous dans
(to 2+) votre siège.

♡☐ Get in your car seats. Asseyez-vous dans
(to 2+) votre siège-auto.

♡☐ Buckle your seat belt. Attache ta ceinture.

C

❤☑

♡☐ Buckle your seat belts. (*to* 2+) — Attachez votre ceinture.

♡☐ Unbuckle your seat belt. — Détache ta ceinture.

♡☐ Unbuckle your seat belts. (*to* 2+) — Détachez votre ceinture.

♡☐ Everyone out of the car. — Tout le monde descend de la voiture.

♡☐ Stand next to the car. — Reste à côté de la voiture.

♡☐ (*to* 2+) — Restez à côté de la voiture.

♡☐ Don't walk. A car is coming. — Ne bouge pas. Une voiture arrive.

♡☐ (*to* 2+) — Ne bougez pas. Une voiture arrive.

the (toy) car — **la (petite) voiture**

♡☐ Where is your car? — Où est ta voiture ?

♡☐ Play with your cars. — Joue avec tes voitures.

♡☐ (*to* 2+) — Jouez avec vos voitures.

C

♥☑

♡☐   Let's play with your cars.   Viens, on joue avec tes voitures.

♡☐   (to 2+)   Venez, on joue avec vos voitures.

♡☐   Here comes the car.   La voiture arrive.

♡☐   Vroom. Vroom.   Vroum. Vroum.

♡☐   You may bring one car with you.   Tu peux emmener une voiture avec toi.

♡☐   You may take one car with you.   Tu peux prendre une voiture avec toi.

♡☐   Put your cars away.   Range tes voitures.

♡☐   **Careful!**   **Attention !**

♡☐   Be careful!   Fais attention !

♡☐   (to 2+)   Faites attention !

♡☐   Pour the water carefully. (slowly)   Verse l'eau doucement.

C

♥☑

♡☐ **Carry me!** **Porte-moi !**

♡☐ Do you want me to carry you? Tu veux que je te porte ?

♡☐ She likes to be carried. Elle aime être portée.

♡☐ He likes to be carried. Il aime être porté.

the class **le cours**

the lesson **la leçon**

♡☐ It's time for your class. C'est l'heure de ton cours.

♡☐ Go to class now. Va en cours maintenant.

♡☐ How was class? Comment se sont passés les cours ?

♡☐ Good. Bien.

to clean **nettoyer**

♡☐ Clean the table. Nettoie la table.

♡☐ (*to 2+*) Nettoyez la table.

C

❤️☑️

🤍☐ Let's clean the table before we put the plates on it. — On nettoie la table avant de mettre les assiettes.

🤍☐ Clean the counter. — Nettoie le plan de travail.

🤍☐ Let's clean the counter before we start cooking. — On nettoie le plan de travail avant de commencer à cuisiner.

🤍☐ Clean the windows. — Nettoie les vitres.

🤍☐ I cleaned up my room already. — J'ai déjà rangé ma chambre.

🤍☐ I cleaned the whole house today. — J'ai rangé toute la maison aujourd'hui.

🤍☐ The house is clean. — La maison est rangée.

CHORE CARDS AND CHECKLISTS FOR CLEANING UP
AT HOME IN THE TALKBOX.MOM SUBSCRIPTION

to clean up   faire le ménage

🤍☐ We need to clean up. — Il faut qu'on fasse le ménage.

C

♥☑

♡☐	Time to clean up.	C'est l'heure de faire le ménage.
♡☐	Clean up the table.	Débarrasse la table.
♡☐	(to 2+)	Débarrassez la table.
♡☐	Please clean up your mess.	Range ton bazar, s'il te plaît.
♡☐	(to 2+)	Rangez votre bazar, s'il vous plaît.
♡☐	You need to clean your room.	Tu dois faire le ménage dans ta chambre.
♡☐	(to 2+)	Vous devez faire le ménage dans votre chambre.
♡☐	You need to clean your rooms. (to 2+)	Vous devez faire le ménage dans vos chambres.
♡☐	Let's clean up your toys together.	Viens, on va ranger tes jouets ensemble.
♡☐	(to 2+)	Venez, on va ranger vos jouets ensemble.

C

♥☑

to close	**fermer**
Do you want me to close the door for you?	Tu veux que je ferme la porte pour toi ?
Close the door.	Ferme la porte.
Close the cupboard.	Ferme le placard.
Close the box.	Ferme la boîte.
Close the drawer.	Ferme le tiroir.

the clothes	**les vêtements**
Pick up your clothes.	Ramasse tes vêtements.
Let's pick up the clothes.	Allez, on ramasse les vêtements.
Take your clothes to the laundry room.	Va mettre tes vêtements dans la buanderie.
Let's take the clothes to the laundry room.	Allez, on va mettre les vêtements dans la buanderie.
Hang up the clothes.	Étends les vêtements.

C

♥☑
♡☐ Let's hang up the clothes. | Allez, on étend les vêtements.

the cloud **le nuage**

♡☐ Look at the clouds. | Regarde les nuages.

♡☐ The clouds are dark. | Les nuages sont noirs.

♡☐ It looks like it's going to rain. | On dirait qu'il va pleuvoir.

♡☐ Those are rain clouds. | Ce sont des nuages de pluie.

cold **froid**

♡☐ It's cold. | Il fait froid.

♡☐ I'm cold. | J'ai froid.

♡☐ I'm freezing. | Je gèle.

C

♥ ☑

	to color	**colorier**
	(with crayons)	
♥ ☐	Do you want to color?	Tu veux faire un coloriage ?
♥ ☐	*(to 2+)*	Vous voulez faire un coloriage ?
♥ ☐	Go get your crayons and coloring books.	Va chercher tes crayons et tes livres de coloriage.
♥ ☐	Do you want a piece of paper?	Tu veux une feuille de papier ?
♥ ☐	Would you like the yellow crayon?	Tu veux le crayon jaune ?
♥ ☐	Please pass me the black crayon.	Passe-moi le crayon noir, s'il te plaît.
♥ ☐	Where did the blue crayon go?	Où est passé le crayon bleu ?
♥ ☐	I need to use the orange crayon.	Il me faut le crayon orange.
♥ ☐	Pass your brother the red crayon.	Passe le crayon rouge à ton frère.
♥ ☐	The white crayon doesn't show on white paper.	Le crayon blanc ne se voit pas sur du papier blanc.

C

❤☑

♡☐　The pink crayon broke. — Le crayon rose est cassé.

♡☐　I can't find the green crayon. — Je ne trouve pas le crayon vert.

♡☐　Your crayon fell on the floor. — Ton crayon est tombé par terre.

♡☐　What a beautiful picture! — Quel joli dessin !

♡☐　Put the crayons away. — Range les crayons.

♡☐　*(to 2+)* — Rangez les crayons.

♡☐　Don't color on the wall. — Ne dessine pas sur le mur.

♡☐　Don't draw on the table. Only on your paper. — Ne dessine pas sur la table. Seulement sur ta feuille.

♡☐　Only color on your paper, please. — Dessine seulement sur ta feuille, s'il te plaît.

> LANGUAGE GUIDES, WALL CHARTS & ACTIVITIES FOR
> ARTS AND CRAFTS IN THE TALKBOX.MOM SUBSCRIPTION

C

♥ ☑

	to comb	**peigner / se peigner**
♡ ☐	Please comb your hair.	Peigne-toi les cheveux, s'il te plaît.
♡ ☐	Let's comb your hair.	Viens, on va te peigner les cheveux.
♡ ☐	(to 2+)	Venez, on va vous peigner les cheveux.

	to come	**venir**
♡ ☐	Please come here.	Viens ici, s'il te plaît.
♡ ☐	(to 2+)	Venez ici, s'il vous plaît.
♡ ☐	Come here right now.	Viens ici tout de suite.
♡ ☐	(to 2+)	Venez ici tout de suite.
♡ ☐	Are you coming?	Tu viens ?
♡ ☐	(to 2+)	Vous venez ?
♡ ☐	I'm coming!	J'arrive !
♡ ☐	We're coming!	On arrive !
♡ ☐	Come in!	Entre !
♡ ☐	(to 2+)	Entrez !

♥☑

the computer	**l'ordinateur**
Do you want to play a computer game?	Tu veux jouer à un jeu vidéo ?
You've been playing computer games all day.	Tu as joué aux jeux vidéo toute la journée.
I need to use the computer.	J'ai besoin de l'ordinateur.
It's time to get off the computer.	C'est l'heure d'éteindre l'ordinateur.
You're grounded from the computer. *(to a male)*	Tu es privé d'ordinateur.
(to a female)	Tu es privée d'ordinateur.

to cook	**cuisiner**
I need to cook dinner.	Je dois préparer le dîner.
Do you want to help me cook?	Tu veux m'aider à cuisiner ?

C

♥☑

☐ (to 2+) Vous voulez m'aider à cuisiner ?

♡☐ **Cool!** **Cool !**

♡☐ **Awesome!** **Génial !**

LEARN TO COUNT, CALCULATE, AND EXPRESS AGE, DATES, & TEMP. IN THE TALKBOX.MOM SUBSCRIPTION

---

to count **compter**

♡☐ Let's count how many ducks there are. Viens, on compte les canards.

♡☐ (to 2+) Venez, on compte les canards.

♡☐ I counted 10 ducks. J'ai compté 10 canards.

♡☐ One. Un.

♡☐ Two. Deux.

♡☐ Three. Trois.

♡☐ Four. Quatre.

♡☐ Five. Cinq.

C

♥ ☑

♡ ☐   Six.   Six.

♡ ☐   Seven.   Sept.

♡ ☐   Eight.   Huit.

♡ ☐   Nine.   Neuf.

♡ ☐   Ten.   Dix.

to cry   **pleurer**

♡ ☐ Why are you crying?   Pourquoi tu pleures ?

♡ ☐ Please stop crying, and tell me what you need.   Arrête de pleurer, s'il te plaît, et dis-moi ce que tu veux.

♡ ☐ The baby is crying.   Le bébé est en train de pleurer.

♡ ☐ The baby won't stop crying.   Le bébé n'arrête pas de pleurer.

learn it!

♥ ☑ *Got it!*

	to dance	**danser**
♡ ☐	Let's dance.	Viens, on danse.
♡ ☐	*(to 2+)*	Venez, on danse.
♡ ☐	Do you like to dance?	Tu aimes danser ?
♡ ☐	I'm a dancer. *(for a male)*	Je suis danseur.
♡ ☐	I'm a dancer. *(for a female)*	Je suis danseuse.

D

♥ ☑

dark　sombre / noir

♡ ☐　It's getting dark outside.　Il commence a faire nuit dehors.

♡ ☐　It's still dark out.　Il fait toujours nuit dehors.

♡ ☐　I am afraid of the dark.　J'ai peur du noir.

STEP BY STEP LANGUAGE GUIDE FOR CHANGING
DIAPERS IN THE TALKBOX.MOM SUBSCRIPTION

---

the diaper　la couche

♡ ☐　We've got a stinky diaper.　On a une couche qui pue.

♡ ☐　Time to change your diaper.　C'est l'heure de changer la couche.

♡ ☐　We need to change your diaper now.　Il faut qu'on change ta couche.

♡ ☐　Your diaper is full.　Ta couche est pleine.

♡ ☐　You pooped in your diaper.　Tu as fait caca dans ta couche.

D

❤ ☑

♡ ☐ You only peed in your diaper. | Tu as juste fait pipi dans ta couche.

♡ ☐ The diaper is still dry. | La couche est encore sèche.

♡ ☐ Poop went out of the diaper, and down his/her legs. | Le caca a coulé de la couche sur ses jambes.

♡ ☐ He / She pooped up his/her back. | Il / Elle a du caca dans le dos.

the diaper bag **le sac à couches**

♡ ☐ I need to pack the diaper bag. | Il faut que je prépare le sac à couches.

♡ ☐ Did you pull everything out of the diaper bag? | Tu as tout sorti du sac à couches ?

♡ ☐ *(to 2+)* | Vous avez tout sorti du sac à couches ?

♡ ☐ Where is the diaper bag? | Où est le sac à couches ?

♡ ☐ I can't find the diaper bag. | Je ne trouve pas le sac à couches.

D

❤️☑️

♡☐ Help me find the diaper bag, please. | Aide-moi à chercher le sac à couches, s'il te plaît.

♡☐ *(to 2+)* | Aidez-moi à chercher le sac à couches, s'il vous plaît.

♡☐ It's in the diaper bag. *(masculine item)* | Il est dans le sac à couches.

♡☐ *(feminine item)* | Elle est dans le sac à couches.

to dig   creuser

♡☐ You can dig in the dirt. | Tu peux creuser dans la terre.

♡☐ Do not dig in the yard. | Ne creuse pas dans le jardin.

♡☐ Dig in the sand. | Creuse dans le sable.

♡☐ What are you digging for? | Qu'est-ce que tu cherches ?

♡☐ Are you digging for treasure? | Tu cherches un trésor ?

D

♥☑

the dirt	la terre

♡☐ Don't play in the dirt. — Ne joue pas dans la terre.

♡☐ There is dirt all over you. (*to a male / female*) — Tu es plein / pleine de terre.

♡☐ I don't mind if they play in the dirt. (*about 2+ males or mixed group / females only*) — Ça ne me gêne pas qu'ils / qu'elles jouent dans la terre.

♡☐ Kids are supposed to get dirty. — Les enfants sont censés se salir.

dirty	sale

♡☐ Take your shoes off, so you don't get the floor dirty. — Enlève tes chaussures pour ne pas salir le sol.

♡☐ You're getting the couch dirty. Take your shoes off. — Tu es en train de salir le canapé. Enlève tes chaussures.

♡☐ Your shirt is really dirty. — Ta chemise est vraiment sale.

D

♥ ☑

♡ ☐ How did you get so dirty? — Comment tu as fait pour te salir autant ?

♡ ☐ Did you play in the dirt? — Tu as joué dans la terre ?

♡ ☐ Your face is dirty. — Ton visage est sale.

♡ ☐ Let's wipe it. — On va le nettoyer.

the dishwasher — le lave-vaisselle

♡ ☐ Everyone load the dishwasher. — Tout le monde remplit le lave-vaisselle.

♡ ☐ Please put your plate in the dishwasher. — Mets ton assiette dans le lave-vaisselle, s'il te plaît.

♡ ☐ Please put your bowl in the dishwasher. — Mets ton bol dans le lave-vaisselle, s'il te plaît.

♡ ☐ Please put your spoon in the dishwasher. — Mets ta cuillère dans le lave-vaisselle, s'il te plaît.

♡ ☐ Please put your fork in the dishwasher. — Mets ta fourchette dans le lave-vaisselle, s'il te plaît.

D

❤️ ☑️

♡ ☐ Please put your cup in the dishwasher.
Mets ton gobelet dans le lave-vaisselle, s'il te plaît.

♡ ☐ I am loading the dishwasher.
Je suis en train de remplir le lave-vaisselle.

♡ ☐ I'm about to start the dishwasher.
Je vais lancer le lave-vaisselle.

♡ ☐ I am unloading the dishwasher.
Je suis en train de vider le lave-vaisselle.

♡ ☐ Do you want to help me load the dishwasher?
Tu veux m'aider à remplir le lave-vaisselle ?

♡ ☐ Do you want to help me unload the dishwasher?
Tu veux m'aider à vider le lave-vaisselle ?

♡ ☐ The dishwasher is clean.
Le lave-vaisselle est propre.

♡ ☐ The dishwasher is dirty.
Le lave-vaisselle est sale.

LANGUAGE GUIDES FOR SETTING THE TABLE AND CLEANING UP IN THE TALKBOX.MOM SUBSCRIPTION

D

❤️☑️

	to do	**faire**
♡☐	You can do it!	Tu peux le faire !
♡☐	*(to 2+)*	Vous pouvez le faire !
♡☐	I knew you could do it.	Je savais que tu pouvais le faire.
♡☐	*(to 2+)*	Je savais que vous pouviez le faire.
♡☐	I can do it by myself. *(for a male)*	Je peux le faire tout seul.
♡☐	*(for a female)*	Je peux le faire toute seule.
♡☐	What are you doing?	Qu'est-ce que tu fais ?
♡☐	I'm going to the bathroom. *(walking there)*	Je vais aux toilettes.
♡☐	I'm making dinner.	Je prépare le diner.
♡☐	I'm cleaning up.	Je fais le ménage.
♡☐	I'm playing.	Je joue.
♡☐	I'm watching a show.	Je regarde une émission.

D

❤☑

	the doll	**la poupée**
♡☐	How is your baby doll doing?	Comment va ta poupée ?
♡☐	You are such a good mama.	Tu es une super maman.
♡☐	You are such a good daddy.	Tu es un super papa.
♡☐	Is your baby sleeping?	Le bébé dort ?
♡☐	My baby is sleeping.	Mon bébé dort.
♡☐	My baby is awake.	Mon bébé est réveillé.
♡☐	Are you taking care of your doll?	Tu t'occupes de ta poupée ?
♡☐	I am feeding my baby.	Je donne à manger à mon bébé.
♡☐	Where is your doll?	Où est ta poupée ?
♡☐	Here is your doll.	Tiens, ta poupée.
♡☐	Your doll is so pretty.	Ta poupée est très jolie.

D

❤️☑️

	Don't…	**Ne… pas.**
♡☐	Don't hit.	Ne tape pas.
♡☐	*(to 2+)*	Ne tapez pas.
♡☐	Be gentle. *(to a male / female)*	Sois gentil / gentille.
♡☐	*(to 2+ / females only)*	Soyez gentils /gentilles.
♡☐	Don't spit.	Ne crache pas.
♡☐	*(to 2+)*	Ne crachez pas.
♡☐	Don't pinch.	Ne pince pas.
♡☐	*(to 2+)*	Ne pincez pas.
♡☐	Don't scratch.	Ne griffe pas.
♡☐	*(to 2+)*	Ne griffez pas.
♡☐	Don't fight.	Ne te bats pas.
♡☐	*(to 2+)*	Ne vous battez pas.
♡☐	Don't throw your toys. Play with your toys nicely.	Ne jette pas tes jouets. Joue calmement avec tes jouets.
♡☐	*(to 2+)*	Ne jetez pas vos jouets. Jouez calmement avec vos jouets.

D

♥☑

♡☐   Don't scream in the house. Go outside to play.   Ne crie pas dans la maison. Va jouer dehors.

♡☐   (to 2+)   Ne criez pas dans la maison. Allez jouer dehors.

♡☐   Don't lock your brother in the room.   N'enferme pas ton frère dans la chambre.

♡☐   Don't lock your sister in the room.   N'enferme pas ta soeur dans la chambre.

♡☐   Open the door.   Ouvre la porte.

♡☐   Don't eat on the couch.   Ne mange pas sur le canapé.

♡☐   (to 2+)   Ne mangez pas sur le canapé.

♡☐   Eat at the table.   Mange à table.

♡☐   (to 2+)   Mangez à table.

♡☐   Don't poke your brother.   Ne donne pas de coups à ton frère.

♡☐   Don't poke your sister.   Ne donne pas de coups à ta soeur.

♡☐   Don't kick.   Ne donne pas de coup de pied.

D

❤️☑️

♡☐ (to 2+) Ne donnez pas de coup de pied.

♡☐ Don't touch. Ne touche pas.

♡☐ (to 2+) Ne touchez pas.

♡☐ Don't make a mess. Ne mets pas de bazar.

♡☐ Be careful. Fais attention.

♡☐ (to 2+) Faites attention.

♡☐ Don't be mean to your (boy) friend. (to a male) Ne sois pas méchant avec ton copain.

♡☐ (to a female) Ne sois pas méchante avec ton copain.

♡☐ Don't be mean to your (girl) friend. (to a male) Ne sois pas méchant avec ta copine.

♡☐ (to a female) Ne sois pas méchante avec ta copine.

♡☐ (to 2+ males or mixed group) (boy friend / girl friend) Ne soyez pas méchants avec votre copain / copine.

♡☐ (to 2+ females) (boy friend / girl friend) Ne soyez pas méchantes avec votre copine / copain.

❤☑

♡☐   Play nicely.   Joue gentiment.

♡☐   (to 2+)   Jouez gentiment.

♡☐   Don't slam the door.   Ne claque pas la porte.
                   Close it slowly.   Ferme-la doucement.

♡☐   Don't leave the water running. Turn the water off.   Ne laisse pas couler l'eau. Ferme le robinet.

♡☐   Don't wake up the baby.   Ne réveille pas le bébé.

♡☐   (to 2+)   Ne réveillez pas le bébé.

♡☐   Be very quiet.   Ne fais pas de bruit.

♡☐   (to 2+)   Ne faites pas de bruit.

♡☐   Play in another room.   Va jouer dans une autre pièce.

♡☐   (to 2+)   Allez jouer dans une autre pièce.

♡☐   **I don't know.**   **Je ne sais pas.**

♡☐   I don't know what you are saying.   Je ne comprends pas ce que tu dis.

♡☐   I don't know why.   Je ne sais pas pourquoi.

D

❤ ☑
♡ ☐   I don't know the answer.   Je ne connais pas la réponse.

♡ ☐   I don't know what happened.   Je ne sais pas ce qui s'est passé.

I don't like...   Je n'aime pas...

♡ ☐   I don't like that toy.   Je n'aime pas ce jouet.

♡ ☐   I don't like to play with cars.   Je n'aime pas jouer avec les voitures.

♡ ☐   I don't like carrots.   Je n'aime pas les carottes.

I don't want...   Je ne veux pas...

♡ ☐   I don't want this doll.   Je ne veux pas cette poupée.

♡ ☐   I want the other one.   Je veux l'autre.

♡ ☐   You don't want to play right now?   Tu ne veux pas jouer maintenant ?

♡ ☐   I don't want to go to school.   Je ne veux pas aller à l'école.

D

the door	**la porte**
Push the door.	Pousse la porte.
Pull the door.	Tire la porte.
Please open the door.	Ouvre la porte, s'il te plaît.
Please close the door.	Ferme la porte, s'il te plaît.
Please keep the door open.	Laisse la porte ouverte, s'il te plaît.
Knock on the door.	Frappe à la porte.

the doorbell	**la sonnette**
Please ring the doorbell.	Sonne, s'il te plaît.
Just one time.	Juste une fois.
Don't keep ringing the doorbell.	Arrête de sonner.

D

❤☑

to go / put down   **descendre**

♡☐   Do you want me to put you down?   Tu veux que je te fasse descendre?

♡☐   Please put me down.   Fais-moi descendre, s'il te plaît.

♡☐   I'll put you down on the couch.   Je vais te poser sur le canapé.

♡☐   I'll put you down on the blanket.   Je vais te poser sur la couverture.

♡☐   I'll put you down on the grass. *(on a lawn / park)*   Je vais te poser sur la pelouse.

♡☐   *(more general word for grass)*   Je vais te poser sur l'herbe.

downstairs   **en bas**

♡☐   Your *(boy / girl)* friends are downstairs. *(about males or mixed group / females only)*   Tes amis / amies sont en bas.

♡☐   Come downstairs to eat.   Descends manger.

D

♥☑

♡☐   (to 2+)   Descendez manger.

♡☐   Go downstairs, and get your blanket.   Va chercher ta couverture en bas.

♡☐   Go downstairs, and get your glasses.   Va chercher tes lunettes en bas.

♡☐   Go downstairs, and get your book.   Va chercher ton livre en bas.

> GET LABEL CARDS FOR ROOMS AND AREAS IN YOUR HOME
> IN THE TALKBOX.MOM SUBSCRIPTION

to draw   dessiner

♡☐ Do you want to draw?   Tu veux dessiner ?

♡☐ What are you drawing?   Qu'est ce que tu dessines ?

♡☐ I am drawing a dog.   Je dessine un chien.

♡☐ I am drawing a dragon.   Je dessine un dragon.

♡☐ I am drawing a princess.   Je dessine une princesse.

♡☐ I am drawing a dinosaur.   Je dessine un dinosaure.

D

♥ ☑			
♡ ☐	I am drawing a house.	Je dessine une maison.
♡ ☐	I drew a picture of my family.	J'ai dessiné ma famille.
♡ ☐	This is daddy.	Ça c'est papa.
♡ ☐	This is mommy.	Ça c'est maman.
♡ ☐	This is me.	Ça c'est moi.
♡ ☐	Thank you for drawing me a picture!	Merci de m'avoir fait un dessin !

LANGUAGE GUIDES, WALL CHARTS & ACTIVITIES FOR
ARTS AND CRAFTS IN THE TALKBOX.MOM SUBSCRIPTION

---

to get dressed   s'habiller

♡ ☐	Please get dressed.	Habille-toi, s'il te plaît.
♡ ☐	*(to 2+)*	Habillez-vous, s'il vous plaît.
♡ ☐	You need to get dressed.	Tu dois t'habiller.
♡ ☐	*(to 2+)*	Vous devez vous habiller.

D

♥☑
♡☐ Do you want me to help you get dressed? Tu veux que je t'aide à t'habiller ?

> CLOTHING CHART & STEP BY STEP GUIDES FOR DRESSING CHILDREN IN THE TALKBOX.MOM SUBSCRIPTION

to drink　boire

♡☐ Drink your water, please. Bois ton eau, s'il te plaît.

♡☐ (to 2+) Buvez votre eau, s'il vous plaît.

♡☐ You drank all of your juice. Tu as bu tout ton jus.

> GET LANGUAGE GUIDES FOR DRINKS AND SPILLING DRINKS IN THE TALKBOX.MOM SUBSCRIPTION

to drop　faire tomber

♡☐ You dropped your toy. Tu as fait tomber ton jouet.

D

♥ ☑

♡ ☐	I dropped the binky on the ground.	J'ai fait tomber la tétine par terre.
♡ ☐	Drop what you are holding.	Lâche ce que tu as dans les mains.
♡ ☐	You dropped your binky.	Tu as fait tomber ta tétine.
♡ ☐	You dropped your wallet.	Tu as fait tomber ton portefeuille.
♡ ☐	You dropped your paper.	Tu as fait tomber ta feuille.
♡ ☐	Did you drop your binky?	Tu as fait tomber ta tétine ?
♡ ☐	Did you drop your wallet?	Tu as fait tomber ton portefeuille ?
♡ ☐	Did you drop your paper?	Tu as fait tomber ta feuille ?
♡ ☐	You are going to drop your binky.	Tu vas faire tomber ta tétine.

the drum   **le tambour**

♡ ☐	Play your drum!	Joue du tambour !

D

❤️☑️

♡☐ Can you tap on the drum with the stick? — Tu peux taper sur le tambour avec la baguette ?

dry	**sec**
to dry	**sécher**

♡☐ The clothes are dry. — Les vêtements sont secs.

♡☐ Let's dry you off. — On va te sécher.

♡☐ Let me dry your face. — Laisse-moi t'essuyer le visage.

the dryer	**le sèche-linge**

♡☐ Help me move the clothes to the dryer. — Aide-moi à mettre les vêtements dans le sèche-linge.

♡☐ The clothes are still in the dryer. — Les vêtements sont encore dans le sèche-linge.

♡☐ Did you move the clothes to the dryer? — Tu as mis les vêtements dans le sèche-linge ?

learn it!

♥☑ *Got it!*

to eat	**manger**
♡☐ What do you want to eat?	Qu'est-ce que tu veux manger ?
♡☐ *(to 2+)*	Qu'est-ce que vous voulez manger ?
♡☐ He / She didn't eat all of his/her dinner.	Il / Elle n'a pas fini son diner.
♡☐ Let me finish eating.	Laisse-moi finir de manger.

LANGUAGE GUIDES FOR SNACKS, DRINKS, MEALS, AND DINING IN THE TALKBOX.MOM SUBSCRIPTION

E

♥☑

	the elevator	l'ascenseur
♡☐	Who wants to push the button?	Qui veut appuyer sur le bouton ?
♡☐	I want to push the button!	Je veux appuyer sur le bouton.
♡☐	(Name) gets to push the button.	C'est (name) qui appuie sur le bouton.
♡☐	Push up.	Appuie sur le bouton pour monter.
♡☐	Push down.	Appuie sur le bouton pour descendre.
♡☐	Go in the elevator.	Entre dans l'ascenseur.
♡☐	(to 2+)	Entrez dans l'ascenseur.
♡☐	Push the button.	Appuie sur le bouton.
♡☐	Push this button.	Appuie sur ce bouton.
♡☐	Push the button with...	Appuie sur le (bouton)...
♡☐	...a one.	... un.
♡☐	...a two.	... deux.
♡☐	...a three.	... trois.
♡☐	...a four.	... quatre.
♡☐	...a five.	... cinq.

E

	English	French
❤☑		
♡☐	...a six.	... six.
♡☐	This is not our floor.	Ce n'est pas notre étage.
♡☐	Stay in.	Reste dans l'ascenseur.
♡☐	*(to 2+)*	Restez dans l'ascenseur.
♡☐	We're here.	On y est.
♡☐	Go on out.	Tu peux sortir.
♡☐	*(to 2+)*	Vous pouvez sortir.

emotions émotions

	English	French
♡☐	How are you feeling?	Comment tu te sens ?
♡☐	Better.	Mieux.
♡☐	About the same.	Pareil.
♡☐	Worse.	Pire.
♡☐	I'm excited. *(for a male)*	Je suis trop content.
♡☐	*(for a female)*	Je suis trop contente.
♡☐	I'm grumpy. *(grouchy)*	Je suis ronchon.
♡☐	I'm happy. *(for a male)*	Je suis heureux.

E

♥ ☑

♡ ☐   *(for a female)*   Je suis heureuse.

♡ ☐   I'm mad. *(for a male)*   Je suis fâché.

♡ ☐   *(for a female)*   Je suis fâchée.

♡ ☐   I'm very mad.   Je suis en colère.

♡ ☐   I'm nervous.   Je suis nerveux.
         (for a male)

♡ ☐   *(for a female)*   Je suis nerveuse.

♡ ☐   I'm stressed.   Je suis stressé.
         (for a male)

♡ ☐   *(for a female)*   Je suis stressée.

♡ ☐   I'm scared.   J'ai peur.

♡ ☐   **Excuse me.**   **Excuse-moi.**

♡ ☐   *(to 2+ or formal)*   **Excusez-moi.**

♡ ☐   **Excuse me.**   **Pardon.**

♡ ☐   Excuse me. May I go by please?   Pardon, je peux passer, s'il vous plaît ?

♡ ☐   Excuse me. Do you know what time it is?   Excusez-moi, vous avez l'heure ?

E

Excuse me.
(If you bump into someone.)

Excusez-moi.

to exercise

faire du sport

I need to exercise more.

Il faut que je fasse plus de sport.

I am going to exercise.

Je vais faire du sport.

Do you want to exercise with me?

Tu veux faire du sport avec moi ?

Daddy is exercising.

Papa fait son sport.

Mommy is exercising.

Maman fait son sport.

> ACTION CHART FOR MOVING + EXERCISING IN THE TALKBOX.MOM SUBSCRIPTION

F

learn it!

♥ ☑ *Got it!*

to fall down	**tomber**
♡ ☐ I don't want you to climb up there. You could fall down.	Je ne veux pas que tu montes là-dessus. Tu pourrais tomber.
♡ ☐ I fell down. *(for a male)*	Je suis tombé.
♡ ☐ *(for a female)*	Je suis tombée.
♡ ☐ You fell down. *(for a male)*	Tu es tombé.
♡ ☐ *(to a female)*	Tu es tombée.

F

❤️☑️

to fart   **péter**

♡☐   Did you just fart?   Tu viens de péter ?

♡☐   Did you fart?   Tu as pété ?

♡☐   Who farted?   Qui a pété ?

♡☐   Someone farted.   Quelqu'un a pété.

♡☐   I farted.   J'ai pété.

♡☐   Gross!   C'est dégoûtant !

♡☐   **Fast!**   **Vite !**

♡☐   Faster.   Plus vite.

♡☐   You run really fast.   Tu cours vraiment très vite.

favorite   **préféré / préférée**
(masculine / feminine)

♡☐   What is your favorite toy?   C'est lequel ton jouet préféré ?

♡☐   Which is your favorite (toy) car?   C'est laquelle ta voiture préférée ?

F

♥ ☑

♡ ☐ This is my favorite picture. (*photo*) C'est ma photo préférée.

♡ ☐ (*a drawing*) C'est mon dessin préféré.

♡ ☐ (*a painting*) C'est mon tableau préféré.

to finish **finir**

(*also*) **terminer**

♡ ☐ Are you finished? Tu as fini ?

♡ ☐ I am finished. J'ai fini.

to fix **réparer**

♡ ☐ Let me fix your toy. Attends, je vais réparer ton jouet.

♡ ☐ I will fix your toy. Je vais réparer ton jouet.

♡ ☐ Your toy cannot be fixed. Ton jouet ne peut pas être réparé.

F

♥ ☑

the flower	**la fleur**
♡ ☐ Look at the beautiful flowers.	Regarde les jolies fleurs.
♡ ☐ Would you like to water the flowers?	Tu veux arroser les fleurs ?
♡ ☐ Let's water the flowers.	Viens, on arrose les fleurs.
♡ ☐ (to 2+)	Venez, on arrose les fleurs.
♡ ☐ I am watering the flowers.	J'arrose les fleurs.

the food	**la nourriture**
♡ ☐ Eat all of your food.	Finis ton assiette.
♡ ☐ Don't play with your food.	Ne joue pas avec la nourriture.

LANGUAGE GUIDES FOR SNACKS, DRINKS, MEALS, AND DINING IN THE TALKBOX.MOM SUBSCRIPTION

F

❤ ☑

	to forget	**oublier**
♡ ☐	I forgot my purse.	J'ai oublié mon sac à main.
♡ ☐	I forgot my bag.	J'ai oublié mon sac.
♡ ☐	I forgot my school bag.	J'ai oublié mon cartable.
♡ ☐	I forgot my backpack.	J'ai oublié mon sac à dos.
♡ ☐	I forgot my homework.	J'ai oublié mes devoirs.
♡ ☐	I forgot my phone.	J'ai oublié mon téléphone.
♡ ☐	Sorry. I forgot. *(for a male)*	Désolé. J'ai oublié.
♡ ☐	*(for a female)*	Désolée. J'ai oublié.
♡ ☐	I forgot what I was going to say.	J'ai oublié ce que j'allais dire.
♡ ☐	I forgot why I came in this room. *(for a male)*	Je ne sais plus pourquoi je suis venu dans cette pièce.
♡ ☐	*(for a female)*	Je ne sais plus pourquoi je suis venue dans cette pièce.

F

❤️ ☑

the fruit   **le fruit**

♡ ☐   Do you want some fruit?   Tu veux un fruit ?

LANGUAGE GUIDES FOR FRUITS AND PUTTING AWAY
FOOD IN THE TALKBOX.MOM SUBSCRIPTION

---

fun   **amusant**

(also)   **marrant**

♡ ☐   Are you having fun?   Tu t'amuses bien ?

♡ ☐   *(to 2+)*   Vous vous amusez bien ?

♡ ☐   Did you have fun? *(to a male)*   Tu t'es bien amusé ?

♡ ☐   *(to a female)*   Tu t'es bien amusée ?

♡ ☐   *(to 2+ males or mixed group)*   Vous vous êtes bien amusés ?

♡ ☐   *(to 2+ females)*   Vous vous êtes bien amusées ?

♡ ☐   I'm having fun.   Je m'amuse bien.

♡ ☐   I'm having so much fun with you.   Je m'amuse trop avec toi.

F

♥ ☑

♡ ☐   *(to 2+)*   Je m'amuse trop avec vous.

♡ ☐   You are so much fun. *(to a male)*   Tu es trop marrant.

♡ ☐   *(to a female)*   Tu es trop marrante.

♡ ☐   *(to 2+ males or mixed group)*   Vous êtes trop marrants.

♡ ☐   *(to 2+ females)*   Vous êtes trop marrantes.

♡ ☐   Playing at your house was so fun.   C'était trop cool de jouer chez toi.

♡ ☐   *(to 2+)*   C'était trop cool de jouer chez vous.

♡ ☐   Thank you!   Merci !

       funny   **drôle / rigolo**

♡ ☐   That was funny.   C'était drôle.

♡ ☐   *(more childish)*   C'était rigolo.

♡ ☐   You're so funny.   Tu es trop drôle.

learn it!

♥ ☑ *Got it!*

the game	le jeu
♡ ☐ Let's play a game.	Viens, on fait un jeu.
♡ ☐ (to 2+)	Venez, on fait un jeu.
♡ ☐ Would you please get out a game?	Tu peux sortir un jeu, s'il te plaît ?
♡ ☐ This is my favorite game.	C'est mon jeu préféré.
♡ ☐ Want to play another game?	Tu veux jouer à autre chose ?
♡ ☐ Let's play another game.	Viens, on fait un autre jeu.

G

♥☑

♡☐   *(to 2+)*   Venez, on fait un autre jeu.

♡☐   We need to put this game away first.   On doit d'abord ranger ce jeu.

♡☐   Put all the pieces back in the box.   Remets toutes les pièces dans la boîte.

♡☐   *(to 2+)*   Remettez toutes les pièces dans la boîte.

the gate   **le portail**

♡☐   The gate is locked.   Le portail est fermé à clé.

♡☐   They can't get in. *(about 2+ males or mixed group)*   Ils ne peuvent pas entrer.

♡☐   *(about 2+ females only)*   Elles ne peuvent pas entrer.

♡☐   They can't get out. *(about 2+ males or mixed group)*   Ils ne peuvent pas sortir.

♡☐   *(about 2+ females only)*   Elles ne peuvent pas sortir.

G

☑
☐ The gate is open. Le portail est ouvert.

the baby gate | **la barrière (de sécurité)**

☐ Who left the baby gate open? Qui a laissé la barrière ouverte ?

☐ Close the gate. Ferme la barrière.

gentle / soft (*masc.*) | **gentil / doux**

gentle / soft (*fem.*) | **gentille / douce**

☐ Be very gentle with the baby. Fais doucement avec le bébé.

☐ (*to a male*) Sois gentil avec le bébé.

☐ (*to a female*) Sois gentille avec le bébé.

☐ Be very gentle with the cat. Fais doucement avec le chat.

☐ (*to a male*) Sois gentil avec le chat.

☐ (*to a female*) Sois gentille avec le chat.

G

♥ ☑

♡ ☐   Be very gentle with the dog.   Fais doucement avec le chien.

♡ ☐   *(to a male)*   Sois gentil avec le chien.

♡ ☐   *(to a female)*   Sois gentille avec le chien.

to give / give back   **donner / rendre**

♡ ☐   Please give me the toy.   Donne-moi le jouet, s'il te plaît.

♡ ☐   Please give your brother the toy.   Donne le jouet à ton frère, s'il te plaît.

♡ ☐   Will you please give my toy back?   Tu peux me rendre mon jouet, s'il te plaît ?

♡ ☐   You need to give him/her the toy back.   Tu dois lui rendre le jouet.

TALKBOX.MOM

G

♥☑

	the glue	la colle
♡□	Just use a little bit of glue.	Mets juste un point de colle.
♡□	That is too much glue.	Tu as mis trop de colle.
♡□	Put the glue on your paper.	Mets la colle sur ta feuille.
♡□	Do not eat the glue.	Ne mange pas la colle.

	Go!	**Vas-y !**
♡□	*(to 2+)*	**Allez-y !**
♡□	Go away.	Va-t'en.
♡□	*(to 2+)*	Allez-vous-en.
♡□	Let's go.	Allons-y.
♡□	*(to 2+)*	Allez-y.
♡□	Go by.	Passe devant.
♡□	*(to 2+)*	Passez devant.
♡□	It's time to go.	C'est l'heure d'y aller.
♡□	It's about time to go.	Il faut y aller maintenant.

G

♥ ☑

It's about time to leave.	Il faut partir maintenant.
We need to go...	Il faut qu'on aille...
You need to go...	Il faut que tu ailles...
I need to go...	Il faut que j'aille...
We are going...	On va...
...to the park.	... au parc.
...to school.	... à l'école.
...to the store.	... au magasin.
...to the grocery store.	... au supermarché.
...to your (*boy*) friend's house.	... chez ton copain.
(*girl friend*)	... chez ta copine.
...to run errands.	... faire des courses.

ILLUSTRATED CHART FOR ERRANDS & SCHEDULING
YOUR CALENDAR IN THE TALKBOX.MOM SUBSCRIPTION

...to the post office.	... à la poste.
...to a restaurant.	... au restaurant.
...to the office.	... au bureau.

♥☑

♡☐ ...to get ice cream. ... chercher de la glace.

♡☐ ...to church. ... à l'église.

♡☐ ...to the doctor's office. ... chez le docteur.

♡☐ ...to the dentist's office. ... chez le dentiste.

♡☐ **Good job!** **Bien joué ! / Bon travail !**

♡☐ Very good! Très bien !

♡☐ Fantastic! Génial !

the grass (*in a field*) **l'herbe**

(*on a lawn*) **la pelouse / le gazon**

♡☐ Come sit on the grass. Viens t'asseoir dans l'herbe.

♡☐ (*also*) Viens t'asseoir sur la pelouse.

♡☐ (*to 2+*) Venez vous asseoir dans l'herbe.

G

♥☑

♡☐ *(to 2+)* *(also)* Venez vous asseoir sur la pelouse.

♡☐ The grass is so green. L'herbe est si verte.

♡☐ *(also)* La pelouse est si verte.

♡☐ *(also)* Le gazon est si vert.

to grow **pousser / grandir**

♡☐ The plant is growing really fast. La plante pousse super vite.

♡☐ The tomatoes are growing. Les tomates sont en train de pousser.

♡☐ You have grown so much! Tu as tellement grandi !

♡☐ Eat your vegetables, so you can grow. Mange tes légumes pour bien grandir.

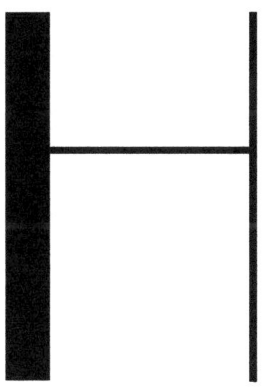

H

learn it!

♥ ☑ *Got it!*

	the hair	**les cheveux**
♡ ☐	Your hair looks great.	Tu as de très beaux cheveux.
♡ ☐	Your hair is all tangled.	Tu as plein de nœuds dans les cheveux.
♡ ☐	Did you brush your hair?	Tu t'es brossé les cheveux ?
♡ ☐	Let's braid your hair.	Viens, on va te tresser les cheveux.
♡ ☐	*(to 2+)*	Venez, on va vous tresser les cheveux.

H

♥☑

♡☐ Let's put your hair up. — Viens, on va t'attacher les cheveux.

♡☐ (to 2+) — Venez, on va vous attacher les cheveux.

♡☐ Let's put your hair up in a pony tail. — Viens, on va te faire une queue de cheval.

♡☐ (to 2+) — Venez, on va vous faire une queue de cheval.

to happen   se passer

♡☐ What happened? — Qu'est-ce qui s'est passé ?

♡☐ What is going on? — Qu'est-ce qui se passe ?

♡☐ Nothing. — Rien.

to hate   détester

♡☐ I hate broccoli. — Je déteste le brocoli.

♡☐ I hate going to bed. — Je déteste aller au lit.

H

the headphones **le casque**

the earbuds **les écouteurs**

Please use your headphones. — Utilise ton casque, s'il te plaît.

Where are your headphones? — Où est ton casque ?

Where are you earbuds? — Où sont tes écouteurs ?

to hear **entendre**

Do you hear that? — Tu entends ?

Did you hear that? — Tu as entendu ?

I heard a noise. — J'ai entendu un bruit.

Me too. — Moi aussi.

Let's go see what it was. — Viens, on va voir ce que c'était.

(to 2+) — Venez, on va voir ce que c'était.

It was a car. — C'était une voiture.

It was a plane. — C'était un avion.

H

❤ ☑

the helicopter   **l'hélicoptère**

♡ ☐   Fly your helicopter over here.   Fais voler ton hélicoptère par ici.

♡ ☐   Your helicopter is going to crash.   Ton hélicoptère va s'écraser.

♡ ☐   I stepped on your helicopter.   J'ai marché sur ton hélicoptère.

♡ ☐   Don't leave it on the floor.   Ne le laisse pas par terre.

♡ ☐   **Hello!**   **Bonjour !**

♡ ☐   Hi! *(to friends and family)*   Salut !

♡ ☐   Good morning! / Good afternoon!   Bonjour !

♡ ☐   Good evening!   Bonsoir !

♡ ☐   Good night!   Bonne nuit !

♡ ☐   **to help**   **aider**

♡ ☐   Do you want help?   Tu veux de l'aide ?

H

♥ ☑

♡ ☐ Do you need help? Tu as besoin d'aide ?

♡ ☐ Please help me. Aide-moi, s'il te plaît.

♡ ☐ Please help your brother. Aide ton frère, s'il te plaît.

♡ ☐ Please help your sister. Aide ta soeur, s'il te plaît.

hot **chaud**

♡ ☐ It's hot. C'est chaud.

♡ ☐ I'm hot. J'ai chaud.

♡ ☐ You're so sweaty. Tu transpires beaucoup.

> LANGUAGE GUIDE FOR DESCRIBING AND DRESSING FOR THE WEATHER IN THE TALKBOX.MOM SUBSCRIPTION

♡ ☐ **How are you?** **Comment ça va ?**

♡ ☐ (also) **Comment tu vas ?**

♡ ☐ (also) **Comment vas-tu ?**

♡ ☐ How was work today? Ça a été au boulot aujourd'hui ?

H

♥ ☑

♡ ☐ How was school?   Ça a été à l'école ?

♡ ☐ How is your day going?   Comment se passe ta journée ?

♡ ☐ How was church?   Comment c'était à l'église ?

♡ ☐ How is your mom?   Comment va ta maman ?

♡ ☐ How is your dad?   Comment va ton papa ?

♡ ☐ How is your (*boy*) friend doing?   Comment va ton copain ?

♡ ☐ (*girl friend*)   Comment va ta copine ?

♡ ☐ Fine.   Bien.

♡ ☐ And you?   Et toi ?

♡ ☐ Having a hard day.   Je passe une mauvaise journée.

♡ ☐ My kids have been really good today.   Les enfants étaient vraiment cool aujourd'hui.

♡ ☐ (*slang*)   Les gosses étaient vraiment cool aujourd'hui.

H

♥ ☑

♡ ☐ My kids have been terrible today. — Les enfants étaient vraiment pénibles aujourd'hui.

♡ ☐ So tired. *(for a male)* — Je suis crevé.

♡ ☐ *(for a female)* — Je suis crevée.

♡ ☐ I got woken up a lot last night. *(for a male)* — J'ai été réveillé plusieurs fois cette nuit.

♡ ☐ *(for a female)* — J'ai été réveillée plusieurs fois cette nuit.

♡ ☐ Really busy. *(for a male)* — Je suis très occupé.

♡ ☐ *(for a female)* — Je suis très occupée.

♡ ☐ Are you okay? — Ça va ?

♡ ☐ I'm okay. — Ça va.

> GUIDE + ACTIVITY FOR INTRODUCING YOURSELF & MEETING OTHERS IN THE TALKBOX.MOM SUBSCRIPTION

hungry   faim

♡ ☐ Are you hungry? — Tu as faim ?

♡ ☐ I'm hungry. — J'ai faim.

♥☑

♡☐ He's acting like that because he's hungry. Il fait ça parce qu'il a faim.

to hurry **se dépêcher**

♡☐ Hurry. Dépêche-toi.

♡☐ (to 2+) Dépêchez-vous.

to hurt **avoir mal**

♡☐ Stop! That hurts! Arrête ! Ça fait mal !

♡☐ What hurts? Où est-ce que tu as mal ?

♡☐ My... hurts. J'ai mal...

♡☐ My head hurts. J'ai mal à la tête.

♡☐ My arm hurts. J'ai mal au bras.

♡☐ My arms hurt. J'ai mal aux bras.

♡☐ My back hurts. J'ai mal au dos.

♡☐ My leg hurts. J'ai mal à la jambe.

♡☐ My legs hurt. J'ai mal aux jambes.

♡☐ My foot hurts. J'ai mal au pied.

H

♥☑

♡☐ My feet hurt. J'ai mal aux pieds.

♡☐ My eye hurts. J'ai mal à l'œil.

♡☐ My eyes hurt. J'ai mal aux yeux.

♡☐ My nose hurts. J'ai mal au nez.

♡☐ My mouth hurts. J'ai mal à la bouche.

♡☐ My knee hurts. J'ai mal au genou.

♡☐ My knees hurt. J'ai mal aux genoux.

♡☐ My stomach hurts. J'ai mal au ventre.

to get hurt   se blesser

♡☐ Did you get hurt? (to a male Tu t'es blessé ?

♡☐ (to a female) Tu t'es blessée ?

♡☐ I got hurt. (for a male) Je me suis blessé.

♡☐ (for a female) Je me suis blessée.

learn it!

♥ ☑ *Got it!*

	to itch	gratter
♡ ☐	My... itches.	Ça me gratte...
♡ ☐	My back itches.	Ça me gratte le dos.
♡ ☐	My nose itches.	Ça me gratte le nez.
♡ ☐	My leg itches.	Ça me gratte la jambe.
♡ ☐	Don't scratch your leg.	Ne te gratte pas la jambe.
♡ ☐	Let's put cream on it.	On va mettre de la crème dessus.

♥☑ *Got it!*

the juice	le jus
♡☐ I want some juice, please.	Je peux avoir du jus, s'il te plaît ?
♡☐ Water the juice down a little bit without him seeing.	Dilue discrètement son jus avec de l'eau sans qu'il te voie.
♡☐ Water the juice down a little bit without her seeing.	Dilue discrètement son jus avec de l'eau sans qu'elle te voie.

GET LANGUAGE GUIDE FOR DRINKS AND SPILLING DRINKS
IN THE TALKBOX.MOM SUBSCRIPTION

J

♥ ☑		
♡ ☐	**Jump!**	**Saute !**
♡ ☐	*(to 2+)*	Sautez !
♡ ☐	Don't jump on the bed.	Ne saute pas sur le lit.
♡ ☐	*(to 2+)*	Ne sautez pas sur le lit.
♡ ☐	Let's jump on the trampoline.	Viens, on fait du trampoline.
♡ ☐	*(to 2+)*	Venez, on fait du trampoline.

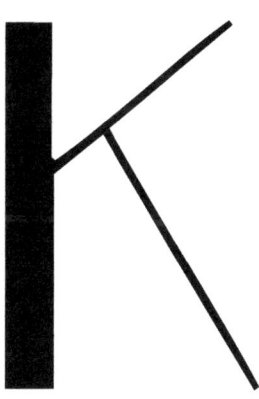

❤☑ Got it!

	the key	la clé
♡☐	Where are my keys?	Où sont mes clés ?
♡☐	Have you seen my keys?	Tu as vu mes clés ?
♡☐	The baby likes to play with keys.	Le bébé aime jouer avec les clés.

	the kiss	le bisou
♡☐	Kisses!	Bisous !

K

❤☑

♡☐   Mom, don't kiss me.   Maman, ne me fais pas de bisous.

♡☐   Give me a kiss.   Fais-moi un bisou.

♡☐   Our baby gives the wettest kisses.   Notre bébé fait des bisous bien baveux.

LABEL CARDS FOR HOW TO USE COMMON ITEMS IN THE KITCHEN IN THE TALKBOX.MOM SUBSCRIPTION

the kitchen   la cuisine

♡☐   I'm in the kitchen!   Je suis dans la cuisine !

♡☐   Get out of the kitchen.   Sors de la cuisine.

♡☐   (to 2+)   Sortez de la cusine.

♡☐   Who made this mess in the kitchen?   Qui a mis ce bazar dans la cuisine ?

to know   savoir

♡☐   I know, mom.   Je sais, maman.

K

to know   **connaître**

Hey! I know you.   Hé ! Je te connais.

I know the answer!   Je connais la réponse !

learn it!

♥☑ *Got it!*

the lake   le lac

♡☐ The lake is so beautiful.   Le lac est tellement beau !

♡☐ We're going swimming in the lake.   On va nager dans le lac.

Later.   Plus tard.

♡☐ We will play later.   On jouera plus tard.

♡☐ We will come back later.   On reviendra plus tard.

L

♥ ☑

♡ ☐ You can have candy later.   Tu auras un bonbon plus tard.

♡ ☐ You can finish later.   Tu finiras plus tard.

to laugh   rire

♡ ☐ It was so funny.   C'était trop drôle.

♡ ☐ We all started laughing.   On s'est tous mis à rire.

♡ ☐ I can't stop laughing.   Je ne peux pas m'arrêter de rire.

♡ ☐ Don't laugh.   Ne ris pas.

♡ ☐ (to 2+)   Ne riez pas.

the laundry   le linge

♡ ☐ The clothes are clean.   Les vêtements sont propres.

♡ ☐ The clothes are dirty.   Les vêtements sont sales.

L

❤☑

♡☐ Let's put the clothes in the washing machine. — On met le linge dans la machine.

♡☐ Let's put the soap in. — On met la lessive dans la machine.

♡☐ Let's start the washing machine. — On lance la machine.

♡☐ Let's start the dryer. — On lance le sèche-linge.

♡☐ Let's move the clothes into the dryer. — On met les vêtements dans le sèche-linge.

♡☐ Let's hang the clothes up to dry. — On étend les vêtements.

♡☐ Let's fold the clothes. — On plie les vêtements.

♡☐ Let's put the clothes away. — On range les vêtements.

> CHORE CARDS AND CHECKLISTS FOR CLEANING UP AT HOME IN THE TALKBOX.MOM SUBSCRIPTION

L

♥☑

the leaf   **la feuille**

♡☐ The leaves are falling from the trees.   Les feuilles tombent des arbres.

♡☐ Here is a leaf.   Tiens, une feuille.

♡☐ Pick up the leaf.   Ramasse la feuille.

ILLUSTRATED NATURE GUIDES + SCAVENGER HUNTS IN THE TALKBOX.MOM ACADEMY

---

to lie   **mentir**

♡☐ Are you lying to me?   Tu me mens ?

♡☐ Tell me the truth.   Dis-moi la vérité.

♡☐ Mom, I lied about something.   Maman, je t'ai menti.

to turn the lights off   **éteindre les lumières**

♡☐ Turn the lights off.   Éteins les lumières.

♡☐ It's not Versailles here!   Ce n'est pas Versailles ici !

L

♥☑

♡☐ Keep the lights off. Laisse les lumières éteintes.

♡☐ (to 2+) Laissez les lumières éteintes.

♡☐ It's time to turn the lights off. C'est l'heure d'éteindre les lumières.

♡☐ Do you want me to turn the lights off? Tu veux que j'éteigne les lumières ?

♡☐ Do you want to turn the lights off? Tu veux éteindre les lumières ?

to turn the lights on   Allumer les lumières

♡☐ Turn the lights on. Allume les lumières.

♡☐ Turn the lights back on. Rallume les lumières.

♡☐ Do you want me to turn the lights on? Tu veux que j'allume les lumières ?

♡☐ Do you want to turn the lights on? Tu veux allumer les lumières ?

♡☐ Keep the lights on. Laisse les lumières allumées.

L

❤☑

to like   **aimer**

♡☐   I like to swim, play with my friends, and stay up late.   J'aime nager, jouer avec mes amis et me coucher tard.

♡☐   I like cookies.   J'aime les gâteaux.

♡☐   I like your teacher. (*male / female elementary school teacher*)   J'aime bien ton maître. / ta maîtresse.

♡☐   (*male / female high school teacher*)   J'aime bien ton prof. / ta prof.

♡☐   I like Michael. (*in love*)   Je suis amoureuse de Michael.

to listen   **écouter**

♡☐   Listen to me.   Écoute-moi.

♡☐   I am listening to you.   Je t'écoute.

♡☐   You are not listening to me.   Tu ne m'écoutes pas.

♡☐   Will you please listen to me?   Tu veux bien m'écouter ?

L

♥☑

♡☐	**Look!**	**Regarde !**
♡☐	*(to 2+)*	**Regardez !**
♡☐	Look at the dog.	Regarde le chien.
♡☐	Look at the tree.	Regarde l'arbre.
♡☐	Look at the table.	Regarde la table.
♡☐	What are you looking at?	Qu'est-ce que tu regardes ?
♡☐	I am looking at a bird.	Je regarde l'oiseau.
♡☐	At nothing. I am thinking.	Rien. Je réfléchis.
♡☐	Look right there.	Regarde là-bas.
♡☐	Look up.	Regarde en haut.
♡☐	Look out the window.	Regarde par la fenêtre.
♡☐	Don't look!	Ne regarde pas !

> ILLUSTRATED NATURE GUIDES + SCAVENGER HUNTS IN THE
> TALKBOX.MOM ACADEMY

L

❤️ ☑

	to lose	perdre
♡ ☐	Did you lose your blanket?	Tu as perdu ta couverture ?
♡ ☐	Did you lose your toy?	Tu as perdu ton jouet ?
♡ ☐	I lost my blanket.	J'ai perdu ma couverture.
♡ ☐	Where did you leave your blanket last?	Où tu as laissé ta couverture ?
♡ ☐	I don't know.	Je ne sais pas.
♡ ☐	Let's go find your blanket.	On va chercher ta couverture.
♡ ☐	I found your blanket.	J'ai trouvé ta couverture.
♡ ☐	You found your blanket!	Tu as trouvé ta couverture !
♡ ☐	I am lost. (*for a male*)	Je suis perdu.
♡ ☐	(*for a female*)	Je suis perdue.

LABEL CARDS FOR HOW TO USE COMMON ITEMS IN
THE BATHROOM IN THE TALKBOX.MOM SUBSCRIPTION

L

♥ ☑

the lotion	**la crème**
Would you like some lotion on your hands?	Tu veux te mettre de la crème sur les mains ?
I need some lotion.	Il me faut de la crème.
Let's put on your lotion.	On va te mettre de la crème.
Put some lotion on.	Mets de la crème.
Rub your lotion in a little more.	Fais pénétrer la crème encore un peu.

loud	**fort**
to be loud	**faire du bruit**
You are too loud.	Tu fais trop de bruit.
Use your inside voice.	Parle plus bas.
Please don't be so loud.	Fais moins de bruit, s'il te plaît.
Would you please say that louder?	Tu peux parler plus fort, s'il te plaît ?

L

♥☑

	to love	**aimer**
	(also)	**adorer**
♡☐	I love you.	Je t'aime.
♡☐	*(to 2+)*	Je vous aime.
♡☐	I love my school.	J'adore mon école.
♡☐	I love riding my bike.	J'adore faire du vélo.

learn it!

♥☑ *Got it!*

the magazine	le magazine
I am reading a magazine.	Je lis un magazine.
Please don't rip the pages out of my magazine.	N'arrache pas les pages de mon magazine, s'il te plaît.
Do you want to look at this magazine with me?	Tu veux regarder le magazine avec moi ?

M

❤️☑️

the magic   **la magie**

♡☐   It's magic!   C'est magique !

♡☐   I did it with magic.   J'ai fait de la magie.

the mail   **le courrier**

♡☐   The mail is here!   Le courrier est arrivé !

♡☐   Did you get the mail?   Tu as récupéré le courrier ?

♡☐   I got the mail already.   J'ai déjà récupéré le courrier.

to make   **faire**

♡☐   Let's make a car with the play dough.   Viens, on fait une voiture avec la pâte à modeler.

♡☐   *(to 2+)*   Venez, on fait une voiture avec la pâte à modeler.

M

❤☑
♡☐   Let's make a   Viens, on fait un
        snowman with the   bonhomme de neige
        play dough.   avec la pâte à modeler.

♡☐   (to 2+)   Venez, on fait un
               bonhomme de neige
               avec la pâte à modeler.

♡☐   Let's make a pizza   Viens, on fait une pizza
   with the play dough.   avec la pâte à modeler.

♡☐   (to 2+)   Venez, on fait une pizza
               avec la pâte à modeler.

♡☐   Let's make a fort.   Viens, on fait un
               château fort avec la
               pâte à modeler.

♡☐   (to 2+)   Venez, on fait un
               château fort avec la
               pâte à modeler.

♡☐   Let's make a wish.   Viens, on fait un voeu.

♡☐   (to 2+)   Venez, on fait un voeu.

♡☐   Make a wish.   Fais un vœu.

M

❤️☑️

	the medicine	le médicament
	(plural)	**les médicaments**
♡☐	It's time to take your medicine.	C'est l'heure de ton médicament.
♡☐	*(plural)*	C'est l'heure de tes médicaments.
♡☐	Did you take your medicine?	Tu as pris ton médicament ?
♡☐	*(plural)*	Tu as pris tes médicaments ?
♡☐	Did you remember to take your medicine?	Tu as pensé à prendre ton médicament ?
♡☐	*(plural)*	Tu as pensé à prendre tes médicaments ?
♡☐	I have to take medicine before I eat.	J'ai un médicament à prendre avant de manger.
♡☐	*(plural)*	J'ai des médicaments à prendre avant de manger.
♡☐	I have to take medicine every day.	J'ai un médicament à prendre tous les jours.

TALKBOX.MOM

M

♡☐ *(plural)* J'ai des médicaments à prendre tous les jours.

the mess	**le bazar**
♡☐ Who made this mess?	Qui a mis ce bazar ?
♡☐ Come over here, and clean up your mess.	Viens ici nettoyer ton bazar.
♡☐ Help your brother clean up the mess.	Aide ton frère à nettoyer le bazar.
♡☐ Help your sister clean up the mess.	Aide ta soeur à nettoyer le bazar.

> LANGUAGE GUIDE FOR CLEANING UP ALL KINDS OF MESSES IN THE TALKBOX.MOM SUBSCRIPTION

messy	**en bazar**
♡☐ The house is so messy.	Il y a un de ces bazars dans la maison !
♡☐ Your room is messy.	Ta chambre est un vrai bazar !

M

❤️☑️

♡☐ You need to clean it before you can go out to play. — Tu dois la ranger avant d'aller jouer.

♡☐ You need to clean it before you can go to your (*boy*) friend's house. — Tu dois la ranger avant d'aller chez ton copain.

♡☐ You need to clean it before you can go to your (*girl*) friend's house. — Tu dois la ranger avant d'aller chez ta copine.

to be missing — **manquer**

to go missing — **avoir disparu**

♡☐ You're missing a sock. — Il te manque une chaussette.

♡☐ One sandwich is missing. — Il manque un sandwich.

♡☐ My son is missing. — Mon fils a disparu.

♡☐ My daughter is missing. — Ma fille a disparu.

M

♥ ☑

	the moon	**la lune**
♡ ☐	It's a full moon.	C'est la pleine lune.
♡ ☐	Where is the moon tonight?	Où est la lune ce soir ?
♡ ☐	There!	Là !
♡ ☐	Do you see the moon?	Tu vois la lune ?

> ILLUSTRATED CHART FOR YOUR CLEANING CLOSET & CLEANING GUIDE IN THE TALKBOX.MOM SUBSCRIPTION

	to mop	**passer la serpillière**
♡ ☐	The floor is disgusting.	C'est dégoûtant par terre.
♡ ☐	I need to mop the floor.	Il faut que je passe la serpillère.
♡ ☐	Careful! The floor is slippery. I am mopping it.	Attention ! Le sol est glissant. Je suis en train de passer la serpillière.
♡ ☐	Please mop the floor.	Passe la serpillière, s'il te plaît.

M

♥✓

♡☐ **More, please!** **Encore, s'il te plaît !**

♡☐ I would like some more. J'en veux encore.

♡☐ Please give me more. Donne-m'en encore, s'il te plaît.

♡☐ Do you want some more? Tu en veux encore ?

♡☐ **the movie** **le film**

♡☐ Let's watch a movie. Viens, on regarde un film.

♡☐ *(to 2+)* Venez, on regarde un film.

♡☐ Which movie do you want to watch? Quel film tu veux regarder ?

♡☐ That is not a kids movie. Ce n'est pas un film pour les enfants.

♡☐ Is this your favorite movie? C'est ton film préféré ?

M

❤ ☑

	the music	la musique
♡ ☐	Let's listen to some music.	Viens, on écoute de la musique.
♡ ☐	(to 2+)	Venez, on écoute de la musique.
♡ ☐	I'm turning on the music.	Je mets de la musique.
♡ ☐	Please turn off the music.	Coupe la musique, s'il te plaît.
♡ ☐	This is my favorite song.	C'est ma chanson préférée.
♡ ☐	Turn up the music!	Monte le son !
♡ ☐	Turn down the music.	Baisse le son.
♡ ☐	My baby loves music.	Mon bébé adore la musique.

learn it!

♥ ☑ *Got it!*

	the nap	la sieste
♡ ☐	You need to take a nap.	Il faut que tu fasses une sieste.
♡ ☐	It's nap time.	C'est l'heure de la sieste.
♡ ☐	It's time for your nap.	C'est l'heure de ta sieste.
♡ ☐	Did you have a nice nap?	Tu as fait une bonne sieste ?
♡ ☐	He didn't nap long enough.	Il n'a pas fait la sieste assez longtemps.

♥ ☑

♡ ☐ She didn't nap long enough. | Elle n'a pas fait la sieste assez longtemps.

♡ ☐ He napped for a very long time. | Il a fait une longue sieste.

♡ ☐ She napped for a very long time. | Elle a fait une longue sieste.

♡ ☐ Stay in your room during nap time. | Reste dans ta chambre pendant la sieste.

♡ ☐ Don't come out. | Ne sors pas.

naughty (*masc.*) | **coquin**

(*feminine*) | **coquine**

♡ ☐ You are being so naughty. (*to a boy*) | Tu es un vrai coquin.

♡ ☐ (*to a girl*) | Tu es une vraie coquine.

♡ ☐ That was naughty. | Ce n'était pas bien.

♡ ☐ You need to shape up. | Il faut que tu te reprennes.

❤☑

to need — **vouloir / devoir**

♡☐ I need to go pee. — Il faut que j'aille faire pipi.

♡☐ I need my binky. — Je veux ma tétine.

♡☐ I need you to listen. — Il faut que tu m'écoutes.

♡☐ You have to wash your hands. — Il faut que tu te laves les mains.

.

♡☐ **Next time!** — **La prochaine fois !**

♡☐ Next time we'll go to the park. — La prochaine fois, on ira au parc.

♡☐ **next to** — **à côté de**

♡☐ Your backpack is next to the couch. — Ton sac à dos est à côté du canapé.

♡☐ You need to stand next to your brother. — Il faut que tu restes à côté de ton frère.

♡☐ You need to stand next to your sister. — Il faut que tu restes à côté de ta soeur.

♥☑

	nice (*masculine* / *feminine*)	**gentil / gentille**
♡☐	You are so nice. (*to a male*)	Tu es très gentil.
♡☐	(*to a female*)	Tu es très gentille.
♡☐	You are so nice to your (*boy*) friend. (*to a male*)	Tu es très gentil avec ton copain.
♡☐	(*to a female*)	Tu es très gentille avec ton copain.
♡☐	You are so nice to your (*girl*) friend. (*to a male*)	Tu es très gentil avec ta copine.
♡☐	(*to a female*)	Tu es très gentille avec ta copine.
♡☐	Be nice.	Sois sage.
♡☐	(*to 2+*)	Soyez sages.

	No.	**Non.**
♡☐	No, thank you.	Non, merci.
♡☐	Never.	Jamais.

N

♥ ☑

♡ ☐   Never again.   Plus jamais.

♡ ☐   No. Don't ask again.   Non. Et ne demande
                                 plus.

♡ ☐   I already said, "No."   J'ai déjà dit non.

♡ ☐   I don't like the chair.   Je n'aime pas la chaise.

♡ ☐   I don't like it either.   Je ne l'aime pas non
                                 plus.

the noise   le bruit

♡ ☐   What is that noise?   C'est quoi ce bruit ?

♡ ☐   Are you making that   C'est toi qui fais ce
                noise?   bruit ?

♡ ☐   Please don't be so   Fais moins de bruit.
                noisy.

♡ ☐   (to 2+)   Faites moins de bruit.

♡ ☐   **Now!   Maintenant !**

♡ ☐   Right this second.   Immédiatement.

to nurse   allaiter

♡□   I need to nurse the baby.   Il faut que j'allaite le bébé.

♡□   I need to nurse the baby in two hours.   Il faut que j'allaite le bébé dans deux heures.

LANGUAGE GUIDE FOR BREASTFEEDING & BOTTLES
IN THE TALKBOX.MOM SUBSCRIPTION

♥ ☑ *Got it!*

	the ocean	**l'océan**
♡ ☐	The ocean is so big.	L'océan s'étend à perte de vue.
♡ ☐	Look how the waves crash on the shore.	Regarde comment les vagues s'écrasent sur la côte.

ILLUSTRATED NATURE GUIDES + SCAVENGER HUNTS IN THE TALKBOX.MOM ACADEMY

O

❤️ ☑️

off(take off / get off / turn off / leave)	**enlever / descendre / éteindre / laisser**
♡☐ Please take your shoes off.	Enlève tes chaussures, s'il te plaît.
♡☐ Please get off the table.	Descends de la table, s'il te plaît.
♡☐ Turn off the lights.	Éteins les lumières.
♡☐ Get off of your brother.	Laisse ton frère tranquille.
♡☐ Get off of your sister.	Laisse ta sœur tranquille.

old (about a m. / f.)	**vieux / vieille**
older (about a m. / f.)	**plus âgé / plus âgée**
eldest (about a m. / f.)	**aîné / aînée**
♡☐ The food is old. (expired)	La nourriture est périmée.
♡☐ That is an old toy.	C'est un vieux jouet.
♡☐ He is older.	Il est plus âgé.
♡☐ He is my oldest son.	C'est mon fils aîné.

O

♥ ☑
♡ ☐   She is my oldest   C'est ma fille aînée.
daughter.

to get on   **monter sur (quelque**
(something)   **chose)**

♡ ☐   Do you want to go   Tu veux monter sur mes
on my shoulders?   épaules ?

♡ ☐   Get on my back!   Monte sur mon dos !

♡ ☐   Get on your bike.   Monte sur ton vélo.

♡ ☐   Do you need help   Tu as besoin d'aide pour
getting on the bike?   monter sur ton vélo ?

♡ ☐   Do you want to go   Tu veux monter sur le
on the rocking   cheval à bascule ?
horse?

to open   **ouvrir**

♡ ☐   Do you want me to   Tu veux que je t'ouvre la
open the bottle for   bouteille ?
you?

♡ ☐   Do you want me to   Tu veux que je t'ouvre la
open the box for you?   boîte ?

♥☑

♡☐ Open the box, please.	Ouvre la boîte, s'il te plaît.
♡☐ Open the door, please.	Ouvre la porte, s'il te plaît.
♡☐ Open the jar, please.	Ouvre le pot, s'il te plaît.
♡☐ Open the cupboard, please.	Ouvre le placard, s'il te plaît.
♡☐ Open the drawer, please.	Ouvre le tiroir, s'il te plaît.
♡☐ Please open this for me.	Tu peux me l'ouvrir, s'il te plaît ?

to get / come out of — **sortir de / descendre**

♡☐ Do you want to get out of the stroller?	Tu veux descendre de la poussette ?
♡☐ Do you want to come out of your crib?	Tu veux sortir de ton berceau ?
♡☐ Do you want to come out of your highchair?	Tu veux descendre de ta chaise haute ?

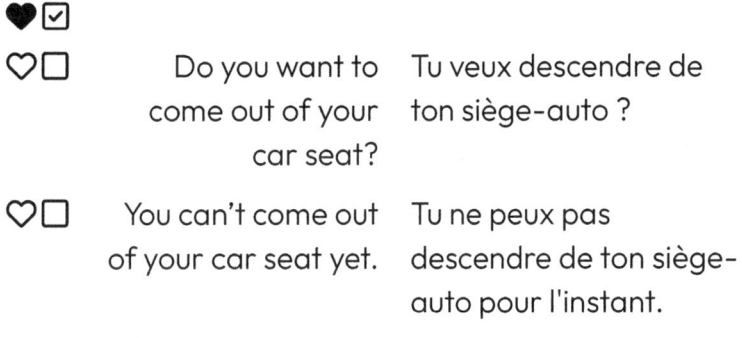

♥ ☑
♡ ☐   Do you want to come out of your car seat?   Tu veux descendre de ton siège-auto ?

♡ ☐   You can't come out of your car seat yet.   Tu ne peux pas descendre de ton siège-auto pour l'instant.

outside   **dehors**

♡ ☐   Do you want to go outside?   Tu veux jouer dehors?

♡ ☐   Let's play outside.   Viens, on va jouer dehors.

♡ ☐   (*to* 2+)   Venez, on va jouer dehors.

♡ ☐   He went outside.   Il est allé dehors.

♡ ☐   She went outside.   Elle est allée dehors.

> GUIDES, CHARTS & ACTIVITIES FOR PLAYING OUTSIDE IN THE TALKBOX.MOM SUBSCRIPTION

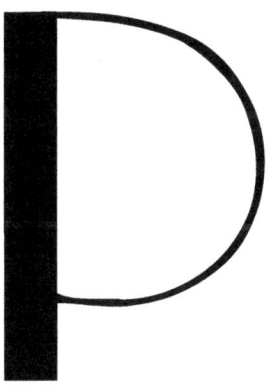

learn it!

♥ ☑ *Got it!*

	the park	le parc
♡☐	Let's go to the park.	Viens, on va au parc.
♡☐	*(to 2+)*	Venez, on va au parc.
♡☐	We're at the park! *(for 2+ males or mixed group)*	On est arrivés au parc !
♡☐	*(for 2+ females only)*	On est arrivées au parc !

LANGUAGE GUIDE FOR THE PARK IN THE
TALKBOX.MOM SUBSCRIPTION

USE FRENCH AT HOME

P

♥☑

♡☐ Do you want to go down the slide? — Tu veux faire du toboggan ?

♡☐ Do you want to go on the swings? — Tu veux faire de la balançoire ?

the path   le chemin

♡☐ Follow the path. — Suis le chemin.

♡☐ *(to 2+)* — Suivez le chemin.

♡☐ Stay on the path. — Reste sur le chemin.

♡☐ *(to 2+)* — Restez sur le chemin.

the pet   l'animal de compagnie

♡☐ What kind of pet do you have? — Qu'est-ce que tu as comme animal ?

♡☐ I have a fish. — J'ai un poisson.

♡☐ I have a cat. — J'ai un chat.

♡☐ I have a dog. — J'ai un chien.

♡☐ I have a hamster. — J'ai un hamster.

♡☐ I have a rat. — J'ai un rat.

P

❤☑

♡☐   I have a bird.   J'ai un oiseau.

♡☐   I have a snake.   J'ai un serpent.

♡☐   I have a lizard.   J'ai un lézard.

♡☐   Did you feed the dog?   Tu as donné à manger au chien ?

♡☐   Please feed the dog.   Donne à manger au chien, s'il te plaît.

♡☐   I fed the dog already.   J'ai déjà donné à manger au chien.

to pet   **caresser**

♡☐   May we pet your dog?   On peut caresser ton chien ?

♡☐   Please do not pet my dog.   Ne caresse pas mon chien, s'il te plaît.

♡☐   *(to 2+)*   Ne caressez pas mon chien, s'il vous plaît.

♡☐   My dog isn't good with kids.   Mon chien n'aime pas les enfants.

♡☐   My dog is really good with kids.   Mon chien est très doux les enfants.

P

❤️ ☑️

♡ ☐ Do you want to pet the dog? — Tu veux caresser le chien ?

♡ ☐ Pet the dog gently. — Caresse le chien doucement.

♡ ☐ The cat likes to be petted. — Le chat aime les caresses.

♡ ☐ The cat hates people. — Le chat déteste les gens.

♡ ☐ Don't pet the cat. — Ne caresse pas le chat.

the phone — le téléphone

♡ ☐ The phone is ringing! — Le téléphone sonne !

♡ ☐ Pick up the phone. — Réponds au téléphone.

♡ ☐ Don't pick up the phone. — Ne décroche pas le téléphone.

♡ ☐ (to 2+) — Ne décrochez pas le téléphone.

♡ ☐ Hang up the phone. — Raccroche le téléphone.

TALKBOX.MOM

P

♥ ☑

to pick up	**ramasser**
Please pick up your toys.	Ramasse tes jouets, s'il te plaît.
(to 2+)	Ramassez vos jouets, s'il vous plaît.
Let's pick up your toys.	Allez, on ramasse tes jouets.
You have five minutes to pick up your toys.	Tu as cinq minutes pour ramasser tes jouets.
Please help me pick up the toys.	Aide-moi à ramasser les jouets, s'il te plaît.
Please pick up your... *(masc. / fem. item)*	Ramasse ton / ta..., s'il te plaît.
(plural items)	Ramasse tes..., s'il te plaît.

the pillow	**l'oreiller**
Do not give the baby a pillow.	Ne donne pas d'oreiller au bébé.
You drooled on my pillow.	Tu as bavé sur mon oreiller.

P

❤️☑️

♡☐ Put the pillows in a pile, and we'll jump on them.   Empile les oreillers, on va sauter dessus.

the plant **la plante**

♡☐ Did you water the plants?   Tu as arrosé les plantes ?

♡☐ **Please.** **S'il te plaît.**

♡☐ *(to 2+ or formal)* **S'il vous plaît.**

♡☐ Say, "Please."   Dis « s'il te plaît ».

♡☐ *(to 2+)* Dites « s'il te plaît ».

to plug something in **brancher quelque chose**

♡☐ Would you please plug in my *(cell)* phone?   Tu peux brancher mon téléphone, s'il te plaît ?

P

♥ ☑

♡ ☐ | Please plug in my (cell) phone. | Branche mon téléphone, s'il te plaît.

♡ ☐ | Would you please plug in my tablet? | Tu peux brancher ma tablette, s'il te plaît ?

♡ ☐ | Please unplug my tablet. | Débranche ma tablette, s'il te plaît.

♡ ☐ | Please don't plug in my my tablet. | Ne branche pas ma tablette, s'il te plaît.

♡ ☐ | Please don't unplug my (cell) phone. | Ne débranche pas mon téléphone, s'il te plaît.

♡ ☐ | Don't touch the outlet. It's dangerous. | Ne touche pas la prise. C'est dangereux.

the poop   **le caca**

♡ ☐ | Look out! Don't step in the poop. | Attention ! Ne marche pas dans le caca.

♡ ☐ | Your stomach hurts? | Tu as mal au ventre ?

♡ ☐ | Did you poop today? | Tu as fait caca aujourd'hui ?

P

♥☑

♡☐ Sit on the toilet, and try to poop. | Assieds-toi sur les toilettes et essaie de faire caca.

♡☐ I need to poop. | Je veux faire caca.

♡☐ The baby pooped in his/her diaper. | Le bébé a fait caca dans sa couche.

♡☐ The baby pooped up his/her back. | Le bébé a du caca jusque dans le dos.

STEP BY STEP GUIDES FOR HELPING LITTLE ONES
WITH THE POTTY IN THE TALKBOX.MOM SUBSCRIPTION

---

the potty   le pot

♡☐ I need to use the potty. | Je veux aller sur le pot.

♡☐ Do you need to go potty? | Tu veux aller sur le pot ?

♡☐ (to 2+) | Vous voulez aller sur le pot ?

♡☐ I need to poop. | Je veux faire caca.

♡☐ I need to pee. | Je veux faire pipi.

P

❤️ ☑️

	a little praise	**un petit compliment**
♡ ☐	You're so smart.	Que tu es intelligent !
♡ ☐	*(to a female)*	Que tu es intelligente !
♡ ☐	You're such a good girl.	Que tu es gentille !
♡ ☐	You're such a good boy.	Que tu es gentil !
♡ ☐	You're so strong!	Que tu es fort !
♡ ☐	*(to a female)*	Que tu es forte !
♡ ☐	You're so fast!	Que tu es rapide !
♡ ☐	You're so cute!	Que tu es mignon !
♡ ☐	*(to a female)*	Que tu es mignonne !
♡ ☐	You're so handsome! *(to a male)*	Que tu es beau !
♡ ☐	You're so beautiful. *(to a female)*	Que tu es belle !
♡ ☐	You're so good at school. *(to a male)*	Tu es vraiment bon à l'école.
♡ ☐	*(to a female)*	Tu es vraiment bonne à l'école.
♡ ☐	You're so good at sports. *(to a male)*	Tu es vraiment bon en sport.

P

♥ ☑

♡ ☐ *(to a female)* Tu es vraiment bonne en sport.

♡ ☐ You always do such a good job. Tu fais toujours du super boulot.

the present **le cadeau**

♡ ☐ I got you a present. J'ai un cadeau pour toi.

♡ ☐ We got you a present. On a un cadeau pour toi.

♡ ☐ You can open your presents. Tu peux ouvrir tes cadeaux.

♡ ☐ I'm opening my present! J'ouvre mon cadeau !

the puddle **la flaque**

♡ ☐ Don't walk in the puddle. Ne marche pas dans la flaque.

♡ ☐ *(to 2+)* Ne marchez pas dans la flaque.

P

♥☑

♡☐ Let's jump in the puddles. Viens, on saute dans les flaques.

♡☐ (*to 2+*) Venez, on saute dans les flaques.

to pull tirer

♡☐ Pull the door. Tire la porte.

♡☐ Don't pull on my shirt. Ne tire pas sur ma chemise.

to push pousser

♡☐ Don't push. Ne pousse pas.

♡☐ (*to 2+*) Ne poussez pas.

♡☐ Did you push your brother? Tu as poussé ton frère ?

♡☐ Did you push your sister? Tu as poussé ta soeur ?

♡☐ Push the door. Pousse la porte.

❤ ☑ Got it!
♡ ☐   **Quick!**   **Vite !**

	quiet	**calme**
♡ ☐	Please be quiet.	Ne fais pas de bruit, s'il te plaît.
♡ ☐	*(to 2+)*	Ne faites pas de bruit, s'il vous plaît.
♡ ☐	Please be quieter.	Fais moins de bruit, s'il te plaît.
♡ ☐	*(to 2+)*	Faites moins de bruit, s'il vous plaît.

Q

❤☑

♡☐ Why is he being so quiet?   Pourquoi il est si calme ?

♡☐ Why is she being so quiet?   Pourquoi elle est si calme ?

♡☐ It's really quiet.   C'est vraiment calme.

♡☐ If the kids are quiet, we know they are getting into trouble.   Quand on n'entend plus les enfants, c'est qu'ils font des bêtises !

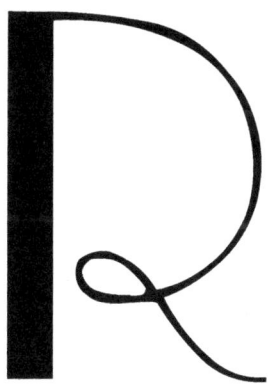

♥ ☑ *Got it!*

the rainbow · l'arc-en-ciel

♡ ☐ Look at the beautiful rainbow. · Regarde le bel arc-en-ciel.

♡ ☐ After it rains, there is a rainbow. · Après la pluie, il y a un arc-en-ciel.

the rattle · le hochet

♡ ☐ Here is your rattle. · Tiens, ton hochet.

♡ ☐ Shake your rattle. · Secoue ton hochet.

R

♥ ☑

	to read	**lire**
♡ ☐	Would you like to read together?	Tu veux qu'on lise ensemble ?
♡ ☐	Let's read together.	Viens, on va lire ensemble.
♡ ☐	(to 2+)	Venez, on va lire ensemble.
♡ ☐	I love reading with you.	J'adore lire avec toi.
♡ ☐	We read together every day.	On lit ensemble tous les jours.

♡ ☐	**Ready!** (for a male)	**Prêt !**
♡ ☐	(for a female)	**Prête !**
♡ ☐	Please get ready to go.	Prépare-toi à partir, s'il te plaît.
♡ ☐	(to 2+)	Préparez-vous à partir, s'il vous plaît.
♡ ☐	Are you ready? (to a male / female)	Tu es prêt / prête ?
♡ ☐	(to 2+ males or mixed group / females only)	Vous êtes prêts / prêtes?

❤️☑

🤍☐ Is everyone ready to go? | Tout le monde est prêt à partir ?

> GET THE GOING OUT THE DOOR GUIDE IN THE
> TALKBOX.MOM SUBSCRIPTION

the river | la rivière

🤍☐ The river is going very fast. | Il y a beaucoup de courant dans la rivière.

🤍☐ The river is going very slow. | Il n'y a pas beaucoup de courant dans la rivière.

🤍☐ Don't go in the river. | Ne va pas dans la rivière.

🤍☐ *(to 2+)* | N'allez pas dans la rivière.

the rock | la pierre
the pebble | le caillou

🤍☐ What a cool rock! | Trop cool la pierre !

🤍☐ Don't throw rocks. | Ne jette pas de pierres.

R

♥☑

♡☐   *(to 2+)*   Ne jetez pas de pierres.

♡☐   I want to take this   Je veux ramener cette
rock home.   pierre à la maison.

to roll   **rouler**

to roll over   **se retourner**

♡☐   The baby can roll   Le bébé sait se
over.   retourner.

♡☐   Let's roll down the   Viens, on descend de la
hill.   colline en roulant.

♡☐   *(to 2+)*   Venez, on descend de la
colline en roulant.

♡☐   Roll the ball.   Fais rouler la balle.

♡☐   Roll the ball to me.   Fais rouler la balle vers
moi.

FUN ACTIVITY FOR ACTIONS, LIKE ROLL + DUCK, IN THE
TALKBOX.MOM SUBSCRIPTION

learn it!

♥☑ *Got it!*

	same	**même / pareil**
♡☐	He got more than I did.	Il en a eu plus que moi.
♡☐	You got the same.	Vous en avez eu autant.
♡☐	You're wearing the same shirt. (*to 2+*)	Vous portez la même chemise.
♡☐	Same here.	Pareil ici.

S

♥☑

the sand	**le sable**
♡☐ He loves to play in the sand.	Il adore jouer dans le sable.
♡☐ She loves to play in the sand.	Elle adore jouer dans le sable.
♡☐ There is sand in my shoe.	J'ai du sable dans la chaussure.

LANGUAGE GUIDES FOR THE PLAYGROUND IN THE TALKBOX.MOM SUBSCRIPTION

---

the school	**l'école**
♡☐ What did you do at school today?	Qu'est-ce que tu as fait à l'école aujourd'hui ?
♡☐ I played outside.	J'ai joué dehors.
♡☐ I took a test.	J'ai eu un contrôle.
♡☐ I drew a picture.	J'ai fait un dessin.
♡☐ I had science today.	J'avais sciences aujourd'hui.
♡☐ I had art today.	J'avais arts plastiques aujourd'hui.

S

♥☑

♡☐   I had math today.   J'avais maths aujourd'hui.

♡☐   I had history today.   J'avais histoire aujourd'hui.

♡☐   I had music class today.   J'avais musique aujourd'hui.

♡☐   I got in trouble.   J'ai eu des ennuis.

♡☐   What did you do?   Qu'est-ce que tu as fait ?

♡☐   I didn't listen to the teacher. (*male elementary school teacher*)   Je n'ai pas écouté le maître.

♡☐   (*female elementary school teacher*)   Je n'ai pas écouté la maîtresse.

♡☐   (*male high school teacher*)   Je n'ai pas écouté le prof.

♡☐   (*female high school teacher*)   Je n'ai pas écouté la prof.

♡☐   I didn't get in trouble today.   Je n'ai pas eu d'ennuis aujourd'hui.

S

♥☑

the scissors	**les ciseaux**
♡☐ Do you want to cut the paper?	Tu veux couper la feuille ?
♡☐ Please cut out a heart for me.	Tu veux bien découper un coeur pour moi ?
♡☐ Good job cutting out a heart.	Tu as bien découpé le coeur.
♡☐ Can you cut a circle?	Tu peux découper un cercle ?
♡☐ Good job cutting out a circle.	Tu as bien découpé le cercle.
♡☐ Cut a square.	Découpe un carré.
♡☐ Good job cutting out a square.	Tu as bien découpé le carré.
♡☐ How do you walk with scissors?	Comment tu marches avec des ciseaux ?
♡☐ Like this.	Comme ça.

LANGUAGE GUIDES, WALL CHARTS, & ACTIVITIES FOR
ARTS AND CRAFTS IN THE TALKBOX.MOM SUBSCRIPTION

S

❤☑

	the seatbelt	**la ceinture (de sécurité)**
♡☐	You need to wear your seatbelt.	Il faut que tu mettes ta ceinture.
♡☐	Please put on your seatbelt.	Mets ta ceinture, s'il te plaît.
♡☐	(*to 2+*)	Mettez votre ceinture, s'il vous plaît.
♡☐	You can't take off your seatbelt.	Tu ne peux pas enlever ta ceinture.
♡☐	I have my seatbelt on too.	Moi aussi j'ai mis ma ceinture.
♡☐	Is everyone buckled?	Tout le monde est attaché ?
♡☐	Buckle up!	Attache ta ceinture.
♡☐	(*to 2+*)	Attachez votre ceinture.

	to see	**voir**
♡☐	Do you see the dog?	Tu vois le chien ?
♡☐	Do you see the bug/insect?	Tu vois l'insecte ?

S

♥☑

♡☐ Do you see the toy?   Tu vois le jouet ?

♡☐ Stay where I can see you.   Reste à un endroit où je peux te voir.

♡☐ (to 2+)   Restez à un endroit où je peux vous voir.

♡☐ If you can't see me, I can't see you.   Si tu ne peux pas me voir, alors je ne peux pas te voir.

♡☐ (to 2+)   Si vous ne pouvez pas me voir, alors je ne peux pas vous voir.

♡☐ Do you want to see what she has?   Tu veux voir ce qu'elle a ?

♡☐ Do you want to see what he has?   Tu veux voir ce qu'il a ?

the shade   **l'ombre**

♡☐ Let's go in the shade.   Viens, on va se mettre à l'ombre.

♡☐ (to 2+)   Venez, on va se mettre à l'ombre.

♥ ☑

♡ ☐   Let's sit in the shade   Viens, on va s'asseoir à l'ombre.

♡ ☐   *(to 2+)*   Venez, on va s'asseoir à l'ombre.

♡ ☐   Stand in the shade.   Reste à l'ombre.

♡ ☐   *(to 2+)*   Restez à l'ombre.

to share *(toys)* **/** *(food)*   **prêter / partager**

♡ ☐   *(Name)* is not sharing with me.   *(Name)* ne veut pas partager avec moi.

♡ ☐   Please share the toy.   Prête le jouet, s'il te plaît.

♡ ☐   *(to 2+)*   Prêtez le jouet, s'il vous plaît.

♡ ☐   You need to share the toy.   Tu dois prêter le jouet.

♡ ☐   *(to 2+)*   Vous devez prêter le jouet.

♡ ☐   The baby doesn't know how to share.   Le bébé ne sait pas encore prêter.

S

♥ ☑

♡ ☐ *(for food or candy)* Le bébé ne sait pas encore partager.

♡ ☐ That was so nice of you to share! C'était très gentil de ta part de prêter !

♡ ☐ *(for food or candy)* C'était très gentil de ta part de partager !

♡ ☐ *(to 2+ for toys)* C'était très gentil de votre part de prêter !

♡ ☐ *(to 2+ for food or candy)* C'était très gentil de votre part de partager !

♡ ☐ Please share with him/her. *(for a toy)* Prête-lui, s'il te plaît.

♡ ☐ Please share with your brother. *(for a toy)* Prête à ton frère, s'il te plaît.

♡ ☐ Please share with your sister. *(for a toy)* Prête à ta soeur, s'il te plaît.

♡ ☐ Please share with him. *(for food)* Partage avec lui, s'il te plaît.

♡ ☐ Please share with her. *(for food)* Partage avec elle, s'il te plaît.

♡ ☐ Please share with your brother. *(for food)* Partage avec ton frère, s'il te plaît.

S

♥ ☑

♡ ☐   Please share with your sister. (*for food*)   Partage avec ta soeur, s'il te plaît.

♡ ☐   I'll share with you. (*for a toy*)   Je vais te le prêter.

♡ ☐   I'll share the toy with you.   Je vais te prêter le jouet.

♡ ☐   I'll share with you. (*for food*)   Je vais partager avec toi.

♡ ☐   I'll share my grapes with you.   Je vais partager mon raisin avec toi.

♡ ☐   He doesn't want to share.   Il ne veut pas prêter.

♡ ☐   (*for food*)   Il ne veut pas partager.

♡ ☐   She doesn't want to share.   Elle ne veut pas prêter.

♡ ☐   (*for food*)   Elle ne veut pas partager.

sharp / pointy   tranchant / pointu

♡ ☐   Careful! The table is really sharp.   Attention à la table ! Elle est très pointue.

S

♥☑

♡☐   That knife is very sharp.   Ce couteau est très tranchant.

♡☐   Do not touch it.   Ne le touche pas.

♡☐   That stick is too sharp to play with.   Ce bâton est trop pointu pour jouer avec.

the shoes   **les chaussures**

♡☐   Put your shoes away.   Range tes chaussures.

♡☐   (*to* 2+)   Rangez vos chaussures.

♡☐   Put your shoes on.   Mets tes chaussures.

♡☐   (*to* 2+)   Mettez vos chaussures.

♡☐   Your shoes are untied.   Tes lacets sont défaits.

♡☐   Tie your shoes.   Fais tes lacets.

LANGUAGE GUIDE FOR PUTTING ON DIFFERENT SHOES IN THE TALKBOX.MOM SUBSCRIPTION

S

❤☑

the shovel — la pelle

♡☐ Use your shovel to dig in the sand. — Creuse dans le sable avec ta pelle.

♡☐ Fill up your bucket using the shovel. — Remplis ton seau avec la pelle.

> LANGUAGE GUIDE FOR HAVING A BLAST AT THE PARK IN THE TALKBOX.MOM SUBSCRIPTION

to show — montrer

♡☐ Show me what's in your mouth. — Montre-moi ce que tu as dans la bouche.

♡☐ Show me what's in your hands. — Montre-moi ce que tu as dans les mains.

♡☐ Show me. — Montre-moi.

♡☐ Do you want me to show you how to...? — Tu veux que je te montre comment... ?

♡☐ Do you want me to show you how to tie your shoes? — Tu veux que je te montre comment faire tes lacets ?

♡☐ I am going to show you how to... — Je vais te montrer comment...

S

♥ ☑
♡ ☐   I am going to show   Je vais te montrer
you how to kick the   comment taper dans la
ball.   balle.

	sick	**malade**
♡ ☐	Are you sick?	Tu es malade ?
♡ ☐	I am sick.	Je suis malade.
♡ ☐	He is sick.	Il est malade.
♡ ☐	She is sick.	Elle est malade.
♡ ☐	They are all sick.	Ils sont tous malades.
♡ ☐	*(to 2+ females only)*	Elles sont toutes malades.
♡ ☐	My family is sick.	Ma famille est malade.
♡ ☐	We've been sick for a week.	Ça fait une semaine qu'on est malade.
♡ ☐	I was sick yesterday.	J'étais malade hier.
♡ ☐	I am getting sick.	Je suis en train de tomber malade.
♡ ☐	I think I am getting sick.	Je crois que je suis en train de tomber malade.

S

❤☑

♡☐ You can't play because you are sick. Tu ne peux pas jouer parce que tu es malade.

♡☐ *(to 2+)* Vous ne pouvez pas jouer parce que vous êtes malades.

♡☐ You can't go to school because you are sick. Tu ne peux pas aller à l'école parce que tu es malade..

♡☐ *(to 2+)* Vous ne pouvez pas aller à l'école parce que vous êtes malades.

♡☐ Do you have a stomachache? Tu as mal au ventre ?

♡☐ I have a stomachache. J'ai mal au ventre.

♡☐ Do you have a headache? Tu as mal à la tête ?

♡☐ I have a headache. J'ai mal à la tête.

♡☐ Do you have a sore throat? Tu as mal à la gorge ?

♡☐ I have a sore throat. J'ai mal à la gorge.

♡☐ Do you have a cough? Tu tousses ?

S

♥ ☑

I have a cough.	Je tousse.
Do you have a cold?	Tu as attrapé froid ?
I have a cold.	J'ai attrapé froid.
Do you have the flu?	Tu as la grippe ?
I have the flu.	J'ai la grippe.
Did you throw up?	Tu as vomi ?
I threw up.	J'ai vomi.
She threw up.	Elle a vomi.
He threw up.	Il a vomi.
Do you have diarrhea?	Tu as la diarrhée ?
I have diarrhea.	J'ai la diarrhée.
Do you have heartburn?	Tu as des brûlures d'estomac ?
I have heartburn.	J'ai des brûlures d'estomac.
Do you have an earache?	Tu as mal à l'oreille ?
(for two ears)	Tu as mal aux oreilles ?
I have an earache.	J'ai mal à l'oreille.
(for two ears)	J'ai mal aux oreilles.

S

♥ ☑

♡ ☐   Do you have an ear infection?   Tu as une otite ?

♡ ☐   I have an ear infection.   J'ai une otite.

♡ ☐   Do you have pink eye?   Tu as une conjonctivite ?

♡ ☐   I have pink eye.   J'ai une conjonctivite.

♡ ☐   Do you have lice?   Tu as des poux ?

♡ ☐   I have lice.   J'ai des poux.

♡ ☐   Not anymore.   Plus maintenant.

♡ ☐   I don't have any left.   Je n'en ai plus.

♡ ☐   I'm all better.   Je vais mieux.

♡ ☐   I feel a lot better.   Je me sens beaucoup mieux.

♡ ☐   I feel better.   Je me sens mieux.

♡ ☐   I'm a lot better.   Je vais beaucoup mieux.

♡ ☐   He is all better.   Il va mieux.

♡ ☐   He's a lot better.   Il va beaucoup mieux.

♡ ☐   She is all better.   Elle va mieux.

♡ ☐   She's a lot better.   Elle va beaucoup mieux.

S

♥ ☑

to sing	**chanter**
♡ ☐ Do you want me to sing you a song?	Tu veux que je te chante une chanson ?
♡ ☐ I love when you sing.	J'adore quand tu chantes.
♡ ☐ You are a great singer.	Tu chantes très bien.
♡ ☐ What are you singing?	Qu'est-ce que tu chantes ?

LEARN TO SING SONGS IN FRENCH IN THE
TALKBOX.MOM SUBSCRIPTION

---

the sink (*in the bathroom*)	**le lavabo**
(*in the kitchen*)	**l'évier**
♡ ☐ Please wash your hands in the sink.	Lave-toi les mains au lavabo.
♡ ☐ (*in the kitchen sink*)	Lave-toi les mains à l'évier.
♡ ☐ (*to 2+ in the bathroom sink*)	Lavez-vous les mains au lavabo.

S

♥ ☑

♡ ☐ *(to 2+ in the kitchen sink)* Lavez-vous les mains à l'évier.

♡ ☐ Put your plate in the sink. Mets ton assiette dans l'évier.

♡ ☐ *(to 2+)* Mettez votre assiette dans l'évier.

to sit   s'asseoir

♡ ☐ Please sit down. Assieds-toi, s'il te plaît.

♡ ☐ *(to 2+)* Asseyez-vous, s'il vous plaît.

♡ ☐ Do not sit down here. Ne t'assieds pas ici.

♡ ☐ Do not sit there. Ne t'assieds pas là-bas.

♡ ☐ Sit next to me. Assieds-toi à côté de moi.

♡ ☐ Sit next to your brother. Assieds-toi à côté de ton frère.

♡ ☐ Sit next to your sister. Assieds-toi à côté de ta soeur.

♡ ☐ Do you want to sit down? Tu veux t'asseoir ?

S

♥☑

♡☐ I need to sit down. Il faut que je m'asseye.

♡☐ *(going to faint)* J'ai besoin de m'asseoir.

♡☐ Let's sit down for a little bit. Viens, on va s'asseoir un peu.

♡☐ *(to 2+)* Venez, on va s'asseoir un peu.

♡☐ Sit on my lap. Assieds-toi sur mes genoux.

♡☐ I want to sit on your lap. Je veux m'asseoir sur tes genoux.

♡☐ Sit on your bottom. Assieds-toi sur tes fesses.

♡☐ *(to 2+)* Asseyez-vous sur vos fesses.

the sky **le ciel**

♡☐ The sky is blue. Le ciel est bleu.

♡☐ There aren't any clouds in the sky. Il n'y a aucun nuage dans le ciel.

❤☑

the sled **la luge**

♡☐ Let's go sledding! Viens, on va faire de la luge.

♡☐ *(to 2+)* Venez, on va faire de la luge.

♡☐ Get on the sled. Monte sur la luge.

♡☐ *(to 2+)* Montez sur la luge.

to sleep **dormir**

♡☐ It's already time to go to sleep. C'est déjà l'heure d'aller dormir.

♡☐ The baby is sleeping. Le bébé dort.

♡☐ Is the baby asleep or awake? Le bébé dort ou il est réveillé ?

♡☐ He is asleep. Il dort.

♡☐ She is asleep. Elle dort.

♡☐ He is awake. Il est réveillé.

♡☐ She is awake. Elle est réveillée.

S

❤️ ☑️

	the slide	**le toboggan**
♡ ☐	Do you want to go down the slide?	Tu veux faire du toboggan ?
♡ ☐	Go down the slide!	Va faire du toboggan !
♡ ☐	I'll catch you.	Je te rattrape.
♡ ☐	Let's go down the slide.	Viens, on va faire du toboggan.
♡ ☐	(to 2+)	Venez, on va faire du toboggan.
♡ ☐	Ready? Go!	Prêt ? Partez !
♡ ☐	Slide on down!	Glisse !

	to smell	**sentir**
♡ ☐	What's that smell?	C'est quoi cette odeur ?
♡ ☐	It smells like… (masc. / fem. item)	Ça sent le / la…
♡ ☐	(plural items)	Ça sent les…
♡ ☐	It smells like coconut.	Ça sent la noix de coco.
♡ ☐	It smells like the dog.	Ça sent le chien.

S

♥ ☑

♡ ☐　　　It smells like poop.　Ça sent le caca.

♡ ☐　　　It smells like　Ça sent le brûlé.
something is burning.

♡ ☐　　　It smells good.　Ça sent bon.

♡ ☐　　　It smells bad.　Ça sent mauvais.

♡ ☐　　　You smell bad.　Tu sens mauvais.

♡ ☐　　　**Smile!**　**Souris !**

♡ ☐　　　*(to 2+)*　**Souriez !**

> COMPLETE LANGUAGE GUIDES FOR EATING &
> DRINKING IN THE TALKBOX.MOM SUBSCRIPTION

snack *(at 4pm)*　**le goûter**

(anytime)　**l'en-cas**

♡ ☐　　　Are you ready for　Tu es prêt pour ton
your snack? *(to a male)*　goûter ?

♡ ☐　　　*(to a female)*　Tu es prête pour ton
goûter ?

USE FRENCH AT HOME　　　221

♥☑

♡☐ Let's eat a snack. On va prendre un goûter.

to sneeze **éternuer**

♡☐ I'm going to sneeze. Je vais éternuer.

♡☐ I keep sneezing. Je n'arrête pas d'éternuer.

♡☐ Why are you sneezing so much? Pouquoi tu éternues autant ?

♡☐ Excuse me. Excuse-moi.

♡☐ Bless you. À tes souhaits.

to snuggle **faire un câlin / se faire des câlins / câliner**

♡☐ Do you want to snuggle? Tu veux faire un câlin ?

♡☐ I want to snuggle. Je veux faire un câlin.

♡☐ Let's snuggle. On fait un câlin ?

♡☐ You are so snuggly. Tu es très câlin.

♡☐ *(to a female)* Tu es très câline.

❤️ ☑

| **the soap** | **le savon** |

♡ ☐ Wash your hands with soap. Lave-toi les mains avec du savon.

♡ ☐ *(to 2+)* Lavez-vous les mains avec du savon.

> STEP BY STEP GUIDE FOR WASHING HANDS & A CHART
> FOR BATHING IN THE TALKBOX.MOM SUBSCRIPTION

♡ ☐ **Sorry!** **Pardon !**

♡ ☐ *(for a male) (also)* **Désolé !**

♡ ☐ *(for a female) (also)* **Désolée !**

♡ ☐ Tell me, "Sorry." Dis-moi pardon.

♡ ☐ Tell him/her, "Sorry." Dis-lui pardon.

♡ ☐ I'm not sorry. *(for a male)* Je ne suis pas désolé.

♡ ☐ I'm not sorry. *(for a female)* Je ne suis pas désolée.

♡ ☐ I don't want to tell him / her sorry. Je ne veux pas lui demander pardon.

S

❤️☑️

to spill   **renverser**

♡☐   I spilled my water.   J'ai renversé l'eau.

♡☐   Careful, or you will   Attention, tu vas
spill your juice.   renverser ton jus.

to spit up   **régurgiter**

♡☐   The baby spit up.   Le bébé a régurgité.

♡☐   The baby spit up...   Le bébé a régurgité...

♡☐   ...on the couch.   ... sur le canapé.

♡☐   ...on my shirt.   ... sur ma chemise.

♡☐   ...on the ground.   ... par terre.

sports   **le sport / les activités
sportives**

♡☐   Let's play football.   Viens, on joue au
football américain.

♡☐   (to 2+)   Venez, on joue au
football américain.

♡☐   Let's play soccer.   Viens, on joue au foot.

S

♥ ☑

♡ ☐   *(to 2+)*   Venez, on joue au foot.

♡ ☐   Let's play basketball.   Viens, on joue au basket.

♡ ☐   *(to 2+)*   Venez, on joue au basket.

♡ ☐   Let's play baseball.   Viens, on joue au baseball.

♡ ☐   *(to 2+)*   Venez, on joue au baseball.

♡ ☐   Let's play hockey.   Viens, on fait du hockey.

♡ ☐   *(to 2+)*   Venez, on fait du hockey.

♡ ☐   Let's go swimming.   Viens, on va nager.

♡ ☐   *(to 2+)*   Venez, on va nager.

♡ ☐   Let's go running.   Viens, on va courir.

♡ ☐   *(to 2+)*   Venez, on va courir.

♡ ☐   Time for soccer practice.   C'est l'heure de l'entraînement de foot.

the star   l'étoile

♡ ☐   Look at the stars.   Regarde les étoiles.

S

♥ ☑

♡ ☐   *(to 2+)*   Regardez les étoiles.

♡ ☐   Here's a star sticker.   Tiens, un autocollant étoile.

the stick   **le bâton**

♡ ☐   What a cool stick!   Trop cool le bâton !

♡ ☐   You must leave your stick outside.   Tu dois laisser ton bâton dehors.

♡ ☐   No sticks in the house.   Pas de bâtons dans la maison.

the sticker   **l'autocollant**

♡ ☐   Here's a sticker.   Tiens, un autocollant.

♡ ☐   I got a sticker at school today!   J'ai eu un autocollant à l'école aujourd'hui !

still   **toujours / encore**

♡ ☐   Are you still eating?   Tu es toujours en train de manger ?

S

♥☑

♡☐ Are you still reading your book? Tu es toujours en train de lire ton livre ?

♡☐ **Please stop.** **Arrête, s'il te plaît.**

♡☐ *(to 2+)* **Arrêtez, s'il vous plaît.**

♡☐ Stop spitting. Arrête de cracher.

♡☐ *(to 2+)* Arrêtez de cracher.

♡☐ Stop hitting. Arrête de taper.

♡☐ *(to 2+)* Arrêtez de taper.

♡☐ Stop fighting. Arrête de te battre.

♡☐ *(to 2+)* Arrêtez de vous battre.

♡☐ Stop screaming. Arrête de crier.

♡☐ *(to 2+)* Arrêtez de crier.

♡☐ Stop yelling. Arrête d'hurler.

♡☐ *(to 2+)* Arrêtez d'hurler.

♡☐ Stop bothering your brother. Arrête d'embêter ton frère.

♡☐ Stop bothering your sister. Arrête d'embêter ta sœur .

S

♥ ☑

♡ ☐ Are you still reading your book? — Tu es toujours en train de lire ton livre ?

♡ ☐ **Please stop.** — **Arrête, s'il te plaît.**

♡ ☐ *(to 2+)* — **Arrêtez, s'il vous plaît.**

♡ ☐ Stop spitting. — Arrête de cracher.

♡ ☐ *(to 2+)* — Arrêtez de cracher.

♡ ☐ Stop hitting. — Arrête de taper.

♡ ☐ *(to 2+)* — Arrêtez de taper.

♡ ☐ Stop fighting. — Arrête de te battre.

♡ ☐ *(to 2+)* — Arrêtez de vous battre.

♡ ☐ Stop screaming. — Arrête de crier.

♡ ☐ *(to 2+)* — Arrêtez de crier.

♡ ☐ Stop yelling. — Arrête d'hurler.

♡ ☐ *(to 2+)* — Arrêtez d'hurler.

♡ ☐ Stop bothering your brother. — Arrête d'embêter ton frère.

♡ ☐ Stop bothering your sister. — Arrête d'embêter ta sœur .

S

♥ ☑

♡ ☐   Stop teasing your brother.   Arrête d'embêter ton frère.

♡ ☐   Stop teasing your sister.   Arrête d'embêter ta soeur.

♡ ☐   Leave him alone.   Laisse-le tranquille.

♡ ☐   Leave her alone.   Laisse-la tranquille.

♡ ☐   Stop jumping on the couch.   Arrête de sauter sur le canapé.

♡ ☐   *(to 2+)*   Arrêtez de sauter sur le canapé.

the street **la route**
(where cars drive)

(including the sidewalk) **la rue**

♡ ☐   We need to cross the street.   Il faut traverser la route.

♡ ☐   Don't walk in the street.   Ne marche pas sur la route.

♡ ☐   *(to 2+)*   Ne marchez pas sur la route.

♡ ☐   Don't play in the street.   Ne joue pas sur la route.

(*to* 2+) Ne jouez pas sur la route.

> LANGUAGE GUIDE FOR NEIGHBORHOOD WALKS IN THE TALKBOX.MOM ACADEMY

the stroller   la poussette

 Is the stroller in the car?   La poussette est dans la voiture ?

Do you want to go in the stroller?   Tu veux monter dans la poussette ?

the sun   le soleil

The sun is really strong.   Le soleil tape fort.

the sunblock   la crème solaire

We need to put on sunblock.   Il faut mettre de la crème solaire.

S

♥ ☑

the sunlight | **la lumière du soleil**

♡ ☐ The sunlight is coming through the window. | La lumière du soleil traverse la fenêtre.

♡ ☐ Open the curtains to let the sunlight in. | Ouvre les rideaux pour faire entrer la lumière.

to swim | **nager**

♡ ☐ Let's go swimming! | Viens, on va nager !

♡ ☐ (to 2+) | Venez, on va nager !

♡ ☐ Do you know how to swim? | Tu sais nager ?

♡ ☐ I know how to swim. | Je sais nager.

♡ ☐ I don't know how to swim. | Je ne sais pas nager.

the swing | **la balançoire**

the baby swing | **la balancelle**

♡ ☐ The baby is in the baby swing. | Le bébé est dans la balancelle.

♥ ☑
♡ ☐   Do you want to swing?   Tu veux faire de la balançoire ?

♡ ☐   I want to go on the swing.   Je veux aller sur la balançoire.

♡ ☐   Would you push me on the swing please?   Tu peux me pousser sur la balançoire, s'il te plaît ?

♡ ☐   Higher!   Plus haut !

♡ ☐   Get me down from the swing.   Fais-moi descendre de la balançoire.

> LANGUAGE GUIDE FOR HAVING A BLAST AT THE PARK IN THE TALKBOX.MOM SUBSCRIPTION

learn it!

❤☑ *Got it!*

the table   la table

♡☐	Go to the table.	Va à table.
♡☐	*(to 2+)*	Allez à table.
♡☐	It's time to eat.	À table !
♡☐	Set the table.	Mets la table.
♡☐	*(to 2+)*	Mettez la table.
♡☐	Sit at the table.	Assieds-toi à la table.

> LANGUAGE GUIDES FOR SETTING THE TABLE AND DINING
> IN THE TALKBOX.MOM SUBSCRIPTION

T

♥ ☑

♡ ☐   Let's color at the table.   Viens, on colorie sur la table.

♡ ☐   (to 2+)   Venez, on colorie sur la table.

♡ ☐   He's hiding under the table.   Il se cache sous la table.

♡ ☐   She's hiding under the table.   Elle se cache sous la table.

♡ ☐   **Take turns.** (to 2+ males or mixed group)   **Chacun son tour.**

♡ ☐   **Take turns.** (to 2+ females only)   **Chacune son tour.**

to talk   **parler**

♡ ☐   Come talk to me.   Viens me parler.

♡ ☐   I need to talk to you.   Il faut que je te parle.

♡ ☐   Your mom wants to talk to you.   Ta maman veut te parler.

T

♥☑

♡☐ Your dad wants to talk to you. — Ton papa veut te parler.

♡☐ What are you talking about? — De quoi tu parles ?

♡☐ (to 2+) — De quoi vous parlez ?

♡☐ Shhh. Don't talk so loud. — Chuut. Ne parle pas si fort.

♡☐ (to 2+) — Chuut. Ne parlez pas si fort.

♡☐ What do you want to talk about? — De quoi tu veux parler ?

the tape **le Scotch®**

♡☐ Here's a piece of tape. — Tiens, du Scotch®.

♡☐ Can you tape the paper? — Tu peux scotcher la feuille ?

♡☐ Can you tape the box shut? — Tu peux fermer la boîte avec le Scotch® ?

T

❤☑

	to taste	**goûter**
♡☐	Taste the soup.	Goûte la soupe.
♡☐	*(to 2+)*	Goûtez la soupe.
♡☐	The food tastes so good.	C'est délicieux.
♡☐	The juice tastes bad.	Le jus n'est pas bon.
♡☐	It tastes like strawberries.	Ça a le goût de fraise.
♡☐	Yummy!	Miam !
♡☐	Yucky!	Berk !

	the teddy bear	**le nounours**
	the plush / soft toy	**la peluche**
	the security blanket *(or any comfort item)*	**le doudou**
♡☐	He always sleeps with his teddy bear.	Il dort toujours avec son nounours.
♡☐	He always sleeps with his stuffed animal.	Il dort toujours avec son doudou.

T

❤️ ☑

♡ ☐ She always sleeps with her teddy bear. Elle dort toujours avec son nounours.

♡ ☐ She always sleeps with her stuffed animal. Elle dort toujours avec son doudou.

♡ ☐ I love my teddy bear. J'adore mon nounours.

♡ ☐ I love my stuffed animal. J'adore mon doudou.

to tell — dire / raconter

♡ ☐ Tell me! Dis-moi !

♡ ☐ *(for a story)* Raconte-moi !

♡ ☐ *(to 2+)* Dites-moi !

♡ ☐ *(for a story)* Racontez-moi !

♡ ☐ Do you have something to tell me? Tu as quelque chose à me dire ?

♡ ☐ *(to 2+)* Vous avez quelque chose à me dire ?

♡ ☐ Tell her / him, "Thank you." Dis-lui Merci.

T

❤ ☑

♡ ☐   (*to 2+*)   Dites-lui Merci.

♡ ☐   Tell her/him your name.   Dis-lui ton nom.

♡ ☐   Tell her/him how old you are.   Dis-lui ton âge.

♡ ☐   Tell me a story, please.   Raconte-moi une histoire, s'il te plaît.

to text (*any app*)   **envoyer un message**

(*phone text*)   **envoyer un sms**

♡ ☐   Did you text her/him?   Tu lui as envoyé un message ? / sms ?

♡ ☐   I need to send a text.   Il faut que j'envoie un message. / sms.

♡ ☐   Who sent me a text?   Qui m'a envoyé un message ? / sms ?

♡ ☐   **Thank you.**   **Merci.**

♡ ☐   Thank you so much!   Merci beaucoup !

T

♥ ☑

thirsty (to have thirst) avoir soif

♡ ☐   I am thirsty!   J'ai soif !

♡ ☐   Are you thirsty?   Tu as soif ?

> LANGUAGE GUIDE FOR DRINKS AND SPILLING DRINKS
> IN THE TALKBOX.MOM SUBSCRIPTION

to throw away jeter

♡ ☐   Throw away your trash.   Jette tes déchets.

♡ ☐   Throw away your wrapper.   Jette l'emballage.

to tie attacher

♡ ☐   I can tie that rope for you.   Je peux attacher cette corde pour toi.

♡ ☐   Can you tie this?   Tu peux attacher ça ?

♡ ☐   Would you tie my dress please?   Tu peux attacher ma robe, s'il te plaît ?

♡ ☐   Tie your shoes.   Fais tes lacets.

T

❤️ ☑️

♡ ☐   (*to* 2+)   Faites vos lacets.

	It's time to...	**C'est l'heure de...**
♡ ☐	It's time to wake up.	C'est l'heure de se lever.
♡ ☐	It's time to get dressed. (*to one or 2+*)	C'est l'heure de s'habiller.
♡ ☐	It's time to brush teeth.	C'est l'heure de se laver les dents.
♡ ☐	It's time to eat breakfast.	C'est l'heure du petit-déjeuner.
♡ ☐	It's time to clean up.	C'est l'heure de faire le ménage.
♡ ☐	It's time to go to school.	C'est l'heure d'aller à l'école.
♡ ☐	It's time to go home.	C'est l'heure de rentrer à la maison.
♡ ☐	It's time to go.	C'est l'heure d'y aller.
♡ ☐	It's time for lunch.	C'est l'heure du déjeûner.
♡ ☐	It's time for dinner.	C'est l'heure du dîner.

T

❤☑

♡☐ It's time to go to bed. C'est l'heure d'aller au lit.

♡☐ It's time to go to sleep. C'est l'heure de dormir.

> LANGUAGE GUIDE FOR SCHEDULING YOUR DAY AND TELLING TIME IN THE TALKBOX.MOM SUBSCRIPTION

the tissue **le mouchoir**

♡☐ Do you need a tissue? Tu veux un mouchoir ?

♡☐ Here's a tissue. Tiens, un mouchoir.

♡☐ Please use a tissue. Utilise un mouchoir, s'il te plaît.

♡☐ Throw your tissue in the trash. Jette ton mouchoir à la poubelle.

♡☐ We are out of tissues. On n'a plus de mouchoirs.

♡☐ I don't have a tissue. Je n'ai pas de mouchoir.

T

♥☑

	together	**ensemble**
♡□	Let's play together.	Viens, on joue ensemble.
♡□	*(to 2+)*	Venez, on joue ensemble.
♡□	Stay together.	Restez ensemble.
♡□	You may play in the backyard together.	Vous pouvez jouer ensemble dans le jardin.

	the toilet / restroom	**les toilettes**
	the bathroom	**la salle de bains**
♡□	I need to use the restroom. / toilet. *(for a child)*	Je veux aller aux toilettes.
♡□	I need to use the restroom. / toilet.	Il faut que j'aille aux toilettes.
♡□	I need to use the bathroom. *(to freshen up)*	Il faut que j'utilise la salle de bains.
♡□	Where is the restroom / toilet?	Où sont les toilettes ?

T

❤☑

♡☐   Let's go to the   Viens, on va aux
            restroom.   toilettes.

♡☐   (to 2+)   Venez, on va aux
                         toilettes.

the toy   le jouet

♡☐   Let's play with the   Viens, on joue avec les
               toys.   jouets.

♡☐   (to 2+)   Venez, on joue avec les
                         jouets.

♡☐   I got you a new toy.   J'ai un nouveau jouet
                         pour toi.

♡☐   We need to get   Il faut qu'on se
     rid of some toys.   débarrasse de quelques
                         jouets.

♡☐   Ow! I stepped on a   Aïe ! J'ai marché sur un
              toy.   jouet.

♡☐   Put your toys away,   Range tes jouets, s'il te
            please.   plaît.

T

	the trash	**les poubelles**
	the trash can	**la poubelle**
♡☐	The trash can is full.	La poubelle est pleine.
♡☐	I need to take out the trash.	Il faut que je sorte les poubelles.
♡☐	Please take out the trash.	Tu peux sortir les poubelles, s'il te plaît ?
♡☐	The trash can smells really bad.	La poubelle sent vraiment mauvais.
♡☐	Throw... in the trash.	Jette... à la poubelle.

	the tree	**l'arbre**
♡☐	Do you want to climb the tree?	Tu veux grimper dans l'arbre ?
♡☐	Look how tall the tree is!	Regarde comme l'arbre est grand !

ILLUSTRATED NATURE GUIDES + SCAVENGER HUNTS IN THE TALKBOX.MOM ACADEMY

T

♥ ☑

to trip   **trébucher**

♡ ☐   Careful. You might trip.   Attention. Tu pourrais trébucher.

♡ ☐   Oh, no. You tripped.   Oh, non. Tu as trébuché.

to try   **essayer / goûter**

♡ ☐   May I try your juice?   Je peux goûter ton jus ?

♡ ☐   Try on your new shirt.   Essaie ta nouvelle chemise.

♡ ☐   Climb the tree. Give it a try.   Grimpe dans l'arbre. Vas-y, essaie.

♡ ☐   All you can do is try.   Tu peux au moins essayer.

♡ ☐   (to 2+)   Vous pouvez au moins essayer.

the TV   **la télé**

♡ ☐   Do you want to watch TV?   Tu veux regarder la télé ?

T

❤ ☑

♡ ☐   (*to 2+*)   Vous voulez regarder la télé ?

♡ ☐   I like this TV show. (*talk show, reality show*)   J'aime bien cette émission.

♡ ☐   (*TV series*)   J'aime bien cette série.

♡ ☐   You've watched enough TV.   Tu as assez regardé la télé.

♡ ☐   (*to 2+*)   Vous avez assez regardé la télé.

♡ ☐   No TV today.   Pas de télé aujourd'hui.

♡ ☐   If you do that, you cannot watch TV.   Si tu fais ça, tu ne pourras pas regarder la télé.

♡ ☐   What do you want to watch?   Qu'est ce que tu veux regarder ?

♡ ☐   You can watch TV for...   Tu peux regarder la télé pendant...

♡ ☐   ...twenty minutes.   ... vingt minutes.

♡ ☐   ...one hour.   ... une heure.

♡ ☐   ...two hours.   ... deux heures.

♡ ☐   Turn off the TV.   Éteins la télé.

learn it!

❤ ☑ *Got it!*

	the umbrella	**le parapluie**
♡☐	We need an umbrella.	Il nous faut un parapluie.
♡☐	It's raining.	Il pleut.
♡☐	Open your umbrella.	Ouvre ton parapluie.
♡☐	Close your umbrella.	Ferme ton parapluie.
♡☐	Shake the water off your umbrella.	Secoue ton parapluie pour enlever l'eau.

U

♥ ☑

	up	**haut**
♡ ☐	The toy is up high.	Le jouet est en hauteur.
♡ ☐	I can't reach it.	Je ne peux pas l'attraper.
♡ ☐	Throw the ball up high.	Lance la balle vers le haut.
♡ ☐	The plane flies up into the sky.	L'avion vole haut dans le ciel.
♡ ☐	Do you want me to pick you up? *(with my hands)*	Tu veux que je te porte ?
♡ ☐	Pick me up! *(with your hands)*	Porte-moi !
♡ ☐	Do you want me to pick you up? *(from school)*	Tu veux que je vienne te chercher ?
♡ ☐	Pick me up from school, please.	Viens me chercher à l'école, s'il te plaît.

	upstairs	**en haut**
♡ ☐	I left my purse upstairs.	J'ai laissé mon sac à main en haut.

U

♥☑

♡☐	I left my shoes upstairs.	J'ai laissé mes chaussures en haut.
♡☐	I left my jacket upstairs.	J'ai laissé ma veste en haut.
♡☐	I left my backpack upstairs.	J'ai laissé mon sac à dos en haut.
♡☐	I'm upstairs.	Je suis en haut.
♡☐	Go upstairs.	Monte.
♡☐	(to 2+)	Descends.

> GET LABEL CARDS FOR ROOMS AND AREAS IN YOUR HOME IN THE TALKBOX.MOM SUBSCRIPTION

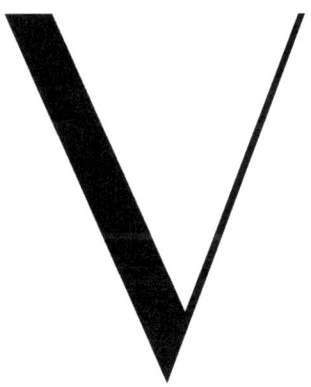

learn it!

♥ ☑ *Got it!*

the vacuum	l'aspirateur
♡☐ I need to vacuum.	Il faut que je passe l'aspirateur.
♡☐ Pick everything up off the floor.	Ramasse tout ce qu'il y a par terre.
♡☐ *(to 2+)*	Ramassez tout ce qu'il y a par terre.
♡☐ The vacuum cleaner came unplugged.	L'aspirateur s'est débranché.
♡☐ Please plug it back in.	Rebranche-le, s'il te plaît.

V

♥ ☑

♡ ☐ Are you scared of the vacuum cleaner? — Tu as peur de l'aspirateur ?

♡ ☐ He is scared of the vacuum. — Il a peur de l'aspirateur.

♡ ☐ She is scared of the vacuum. — Elle a peur de l'aspirateur.

♡ ☐ Go in the other room. — Va dans l'autre pièce.

♡ ☐ (to 2+) — Allez dans l'autre pièce.

♡ ☐ I am going to vacuum. — Je vais passer l'aspirateur.

♡ ☐ I can't hear you. — Je ne t'entends pas.

♡ ☐ The vacuum is too loud. — L'aspirateur fait trop de bruit.

the video game — le jeu vidéo

♡ ☐ Which video game do you want to play? — A quel jeu vidéo tu veux jouer ?

♡ ☐ Let's play video games. — Viens, on joue aux jeux vidéo.

♡ ☐ (to 2+) — Venez, on joue aux jeux vidéo.

V

♥ ☑
♡ ☐ Please turn off your   Coupe ton jeu, s'il te
          video games.   plaît.

♡ ☐   (to 2+)   Coupez votre jeu, s'il
                              vous plaît.

learn it!

♥ ☑ *Got it!*

	the wagon	**le chariot**
♡ ☐	Get in the wagon.	Monte dans le chariot.
	(to 2+)	Montez dans le chariot.
♡ ☐	I'll pull the wagon.	Je vais pousser le chariot.

	Wait.	**Attends.**
♡ ☐	*(to 2+)*	Attendez.
♡ ☐	Wait for me.	Attends-moi.
♡ ☐	*(to 2+)*	Attendez-moi.

W

♥ ☑

♡ ☐ Wait one second. Attends une seconde.

♡ ☐ Wait one minute. Attends une minute.

♡ ☐ One moment. Une minute.

♡ ☐ You need to wait five minutes. Il faut que tu attendes cinq minutes.

♡ ☐ (to 2+) Il faut que vous attendiez cinq minutes.

♡ ☐ We waited for... On a attendu pendant...

♡ ☐ We've been waiting for... On attend depuis...

♡ ☐ ...five minutes. ... cinq minutes.

♡ ☐ ...ten minutes. ... dix minutes.

♡ ☐ ...fifteen minutes. ... quinze minutes.

♡ ☐ ...twenty minutes. ... vingt minutes.

♡ ☐ **Wake up.** **Réveille-toi.**

♡ ☐ (to 2+) **Réveillez-vous.**

♡ ☐ It's time to wake up. C'est l'heure de se réveiller.

♡ ☐ It's time to get up. C'est l'heure de se lever.

W

♥ ☑

♡ ☐   It's not time to wake up yet.   Ce n'est pas encore l'heure de se réveiller.

♡ ☐   It's not time to get up yet.   Ce n'est pas encore l'heure de se lever.

♡ ☐   Please don't wake up...   S'il te plaît, ne réveille pas...

♡ ☐   ...your brother.   ... ton frère.

♡ ☐   ...your sister.   ... ta sœur.

♡ ☐   ...your father.   ... ton père.

♡ ☐   ...your mother.   ... ta mère.

♡ ☐   ...the baby.   ... le bébé

♡ ☐   Please don't wake me up.   Ne me réveille pas, s'il te plaît.

♡ ☐   (to 2+)   Ne me réveillez pas, s'il vous plaît.

♡ ☐   I need to take a nap.   J'ai besoin de faire une sieste.

♡ ☐   He woke up early from his nap.   Il s'est réveillé tôt de sa sieste.

♡ ☐   She woke up early from her nap.   Elle s'est réveillée tôt de sa sieste.

to walk   **marcher**

Let's go on a walk.   Viens, on va faire une promenade.

(to 2+)   Venez, on va faire une promenade.

Don't be lazy. Walk.   Arrête de traîner. Avance.

Is your baby walking yet?   Ton bébé marche déjà ?

The baby can walk.   Le bébé marche.

The baby can't walk.   Le bébé ne marche pas encore.

GUIDES FOR WALKS, PLUS CHARTS FOR TALKING ABOUT WHAT YOU SEE, IN THE TALKBOX.MOM ACADEMY

---

to want   **vouloir**

Do you want that toy?   Tu veux ce jouet ?

What do you want?   Qu'est-ce que tu veux ?

W

♥ ☑
♡ ☐   I want a cookie, please.   Je peux avoir un gâteau, s'il te plaît ?

♡ ☐   I can't give you what you want if you are crying.   Je ne peux pas te donner ce que tu veux si tu pleures.

to wash   laver

♡ ☐   Wash your face.   Lave-toi le visage.

♡ ☐   Wash your hands.   Lave-toi les mains.

♡ ☐   *(to 2+)*   Lavez-vous les mains.

♡ ☐   Did you wash your hands?   Tu t'es lavé les mains ?

♡ ☐   Wash your hands again.   Lave-toi encore les mains.

> STEP BY STEP GUIDE FOR WASHING HANDS (THAT GOES ABOVE THE SINK) IN THE TALKBOX.MOM SUBSCRIPTION

♥☑

to wash the dishes	**faire la vaisselle**
Wash your plate off, please.	Lave ton assiette, s'il te plaît.
Wash your plates off, please. (*to 2+*)	Lavez vos assiettes, s'il vous plaît.
Please wash the dishes.	Fais la vaisselle, s'il te plaît.
I need to wash the dishes.	Il faut que je fasse la vaisselle.
I washed the dishes.	J'ai fait la vaisselle.
Could you help (*name*) wash the dishes?	Tu peux aider (*name*) à faire la vaisselle ?
(*to 2+*)	Vous pouvez aider (*name*) à faire la vaisselle ?
Help (*name*) wash the dishes, please.	Aide (*name*) à faire la vaisselle, s'il te plaît.
(*to 2+*)	Aidez (*name*) à faire la vaisselle, s'il vous plaît.
Help me wash the dishes, please.	Aide-moi à faire la vaisselle, s'il te plaît.
(*to 2+*)	Aidez-moi à faire la vaisselle, s'il vous plaît.

W

❤️ ☑️

the watch	**la montre**
♡ ☐ Where is my watch?	Où est ma montre ?
♡ ☐ Where did you put my watch?	Où tu as mis ma montre ?
♡ ☐ Do you want to play with my watch?	Tu veux jouer avec ma montre ?

> GUIDES FOR TELLING TIME TO SCHEDULE AND ARRIVE
> AT ACTIVITIES IN THE TALKBOX.MOM SUBSCRIPTION

to watch	**regarder / surveiller**
♡ ☐ You may watch TV now.	Tu peux regarder la télé maintenant.
♡ ☐ (to 2+)	Vous pouvez regarder la télé maintenant.
♡ ☐ What are you watching?	Qu'est-ce que tu regardes ?
♡ ☐ (to 2+)	Qu'est-ce que vous regardez ?
♡ ☐ A show.	Une émission.
♡ ☐ A movie.	Un film.

W

♥ ☑

♡ ☐ I am watching you.   Je te regarde.

♡ ☐ Will you watch the kids tonight?   Tu veux bien garder les enfants ce soir ?

♡ ☐ I'll watch the kids while you run errands.   Je garderai les enfants quand tu iras faire les courses.

the water   **l'eau**

♡ ☐ Do you want some water?   Tu veux de l'eau ?

♡ ☐ (to 2+)   Vous voulez de l'eau ?

♡ ☐ Look at the water!   Regarde l'eau !

♡ ☐ (to 2+)   Regardez l'eau !

♡ ☐ Don't go in the water.   Ne va pas dans l'eau.

♡ ☐ (to 2+)   N'allez pas dans l'eau.

♡ ☐ Don't step in the water.   Ne mets pas les pieds dans l'eau.

♡ ☐ (to 2+)   Ne mettez pas les pieds dans l'eau.

W

♥ ☑

the weather — le temps

♡ ☐	What's the weather today?	Quel temps il fait aujourd'hui ?
♡ ☐	It's raining.	Il pleut.
♡ ☐	It's snowing.	Il neige.
♡ ☐	It's hailing.	Il grêle.
♡ ☐	It's sunny.	Il fait beau.
♡ ☐	It's cloudy.	Il fait nuageux.
♡ ☐	(*The sky is covered.*)	Le ciel est couvert.
♡ ☐	There's a storm.	Il y a de l'orage.

> LANGUAGE GUIDE FOR DESCRIBING & DRESSING FOR
> THE WEATHER IN THE TALKBOX.MOM SUBSCRIPTION

♡ ☐	**Welcome!**	**Bienvenue !**
♡ ☐	Welcome to our house.	Bienvenue chez nous.
♡ ☐	Welcome home!	Bienvenue à la maison !
♡ ☐	Thank you!	Merci !
♡ ☐	You're welcome.	De rien.

USE FRENCH AT HOME

W

♥ ☑
♡ ☐   *(also)*   Je t'en prie.

	wet	**mouillé / mouillée**
♡ ☐	Why is the floor all wet?	Pourquoi le sol est mouillé ?
♡ ☐	Why is your bottom wet?	Pourquoi tes fesses sont mouillées ?
♡ ☐	Why are his/her pants wet?	Pourquoi son pantalon est mouillé ?

♡ ☐   **What? / Yes?**   **Pardon ? / Quoi ?**
(As in, " What did you say?")

	the wheel	**la roue**
♡ ☐	Your bike has...	Ton vélo a...
♡ ☐	...two wheels.	... deux roues.
♡ ☐	...three wheels.	... trois roues.
♡ ☐	...four wheels.	... quatre roues.

W

❤☑
♡☐   He rides a bike with   Il fait du vélo avec des
         training wheels.   petites roues.

♡☐   He rides a bike   Il fait du vélo sans les
         without training   petites roues.
                wheels.

to whisper   **chuchoter**

♡☐   Will you please   Tu peux chuchoter, s'il
              whisper?   te plaît ?

♡☐   Please whisper.   Chuchote, s'il te plaît.

♡☐   What are you   Qu'est-ce que tu
         whispering about?   chuchotes ?

to win   **gagner**

♡☐   I'm going to win!   Je vais gagner !

♡☐   I won!   J'ai gagné !

♡☐   Let your sister win   Laisse ta sœur gagner
             this time.   cette fois-ci.

♡☐   Let your brother win   Laisse ton frère gagner
             this time.   cette fois-ci.

♥ ☑

the wind   le vent

♡ □   It's very windy.   Il y a beaucoup de vent.

♡ □   The wind is blowing.   Le vent souffle.

♡ □   That was the wind.   C'était le vent.

to worry   s'inquiéter

♡ □   Don't worry about it.   Il fait nuageux.

♡ □   I'm worried.   Je suis inquiet.
    (for a male)

♡ □   *(for a female)*   Je suis inquiète.

♡ □   *(also)*   Je m'inquiète.

♡ □   I'm worried about...   Je m'inquiète pour...

♡ □   I'm worried about my   Je m'inquiète pour mon
    test.   examen.

learn it!

♥☑ *Got it!*

the yard	**le jardin**

♡☐ Let's play in the yard. — Viens, on va jouer dans le jardin.

♡☐ (*to 2+*) — Venez, on va jouer dans le jardin.

♡☐ Go play in the yard. — Va jouer dans le jardin.

to yell	**crier**

♡☐ Don't yell in the house. — Ne crie pas dans la maison.

Y

♥☑
♡☐   *(to 2+)*   Ne criez pas dans la maison.

♡☐   Yell to your brother to come in.   Appelle ton frère et dis-lui de rentrer.

♡☐   Yell to your sister to come in.   Appelle ta sœur et dis-lui de rentrer.

♡☐   **Yes.**   **Oui.**

♡☐   Of course.   Bien sûr.

♡☐   *(also)*   Evidemment.

♡☐   Absolutely.   Tout à fait.

♡☐   *(also)*   Absolument.

♥☑ *Got it!*

	the zipper	la fermeture éclair
♡☐	Zip up your zipper.	Remonte ta fermeture éclair.
♡☐	Your fly is down.	Ta braguette est ouverte.

> GUIDE FOR FIXING COMMON DRESSING MISHAPS, LIKE
> UNZIPPED PANTS, IN THE TALKBOX.MOM SUBSCRIPTION

	the zoo	le zoo
♡☐	We're going to the zoo today.	Aujourd'hui, on va au zoo.

Helping Children Reply Back

"I want my child to use their phrases without prompting."

Then let's jump in and get one thing straight: the word "education" comes from the word "educe," which means to "bring out" or "draw forth."

It does not mean to pack in.

This means that goals like:

❌ memorizing a phrase

❌ perfect pronunciation

❌ learning everything at once

❌ remembering right away

aren't actually educational goals.

Notice how all of these "goals" focus on the <u>result.</u> These "goals" are focused on packing information into a child for them to perform perfectly. With closer examination, we see "wishes" masquerading as "goals."

Wishes are dreams that are outside of your control.

For example, you can't control if your child memorizes something, and you can't control if your child's pronunciation is perfect. You can really, really want it, or even grumble, "I will *make* them do it!" But you cannot control it.

Goals on the other hand are dreams that are in your control. What's inside your control? The PROCESS that sets your child in the direction of the wish. This is 100% inside your control.

This means the way that you carry out your Practice Sessions changes everything. If you're skipping steps and nitpicking (aka focused on the results instead of the process), you're going to run into trouble.

Remember, "a horse that wants to race will always beat a horse that is forced."

I see this over and over again. Parents who focus on the process pass up the trajectory of what they previously planned to achieve. Whereas parents who focus on the results carry a level of anxiety with them that increases as the disparity between the wish and reality increases over time. This anxiety weighs on the child or comes out in outbursts from the parent, creating a teary-eyed mess.

Learning to use a language with your family should be a place of connection and joy. It should be an endearing memory. So if you've made French a chore instead of a pleasure, it's time to reset and refocus. It's not too late. You'll be able to create healing experiences as you focus on a true education.

There are four very effective ways to educate or draw forth:

☑ Inspiring
☑ Enticing
☑ Loving
☑ Rewarding

Note bribing is giving someone something to stop bad behavior. Rewarding is having a clearly stated reward and working towards that reward to encourage good behavior.

Your goal as you create an immersion environment in your home is to help draw forth the desire for your child to use the language. For some parents, this can be a piece of cake with their child. For those same parents, it can be a whole different story with another one of their kids.

With that said, you are the best, most invested person to help your child. As you read through the ideas in each of these categories below, I want you to try the ones that you think will speak to your child or, at least, be inspired by these. And if you fail, fail fast and try again.

Inspiring - *create a positive feeling in a person*

• Model practicing and using the phrases yourself with excitement and enthusiasm.

- Give your child a sense of control: Do you want to practice this phrase or this phrase? You're in charge of playing the audio. You're in charge of assigning emotions.

- Share the new phrases you've learned with trusted family and friends, proudly showcasing your skills.

- Change your scenery to somewhere you don't typically practice.

Enticing - *attract or tempt by offering pleasure or advantage*

- If your child asks for a favorite snack nicely in the foreign language, happily give it to them.

- If your child asks for your service nicely in the foreign language, serve your child.

- Make your Practice Session fun with your child's interests in mind.

- Eat food or dessert from the country as you practice or serve a favorite drink.

- Put the language guides at your child's eye level.

Loving - *consider how your child feels loved*

- Words of affirmation: Use effective praise that focuses on the process—not the result.

- Quality time: Have a special practice session or review time with one child.

- Physical touch: Snuggle as you practice. High-five

or hug after trying a phrase.

- Acts of service: After practicing, surprise your child by cleaning something for them, solving a problem for them, or making a snack for them.

- Receiving gifts: A special present to practice phrases in a new box or challenge.

Rewarding - *choose a reward and work towards it*

- A movie night out together or a fun restaurant after completing 10 practice sessions.

- Extra video game time, time with friends, or other activity time per practice session.

- A trip with one child or the whole family to a country that speaks the language.

As you work through the TalkBox.Mom Program, you'll notice that our program revolves around true educational goals and not wishes. This is why our families succeed, and you can too!

Getting Outside your Comfort Zone

Don't fall into the trap that your French needs to be at a certain level to talk with other French speakers. Quite the opposite. You should definitely take advantage of solid opportunities to practice what you can say and learn from others as you talk. These experiences will stretch you, helping you to continue to grow.

However, these humbling experiences can feel extremely frightening. In the face of **speaking** *to get better at* **speaking** *another language*, many language learners retreat and engage in shadow activities.

Shadow activities, as coined by Stephen Pressfield, are activities that lie in the shadow of your goal. These activities seem like you're working toward your goal, but you're actually avoiding what will really help you to improve.

Notice above that I wrote "speaking" to get better at "speaking." Shadow activities would be doing everything but "speaking" to get better at "speaking."

Like, memorizing vocabulary words, writing, doing grammar activities, and reading.

These activities will help you get better at *those* activities, but they won't push you further towards your goal of **speaking** another language like actually **speaking** another language will.

And when you improve your ability to speak, you fast track your vocabulary growth as well as your ability to gain fluency in reading, writing, and grammar.

Wait. Why is that? Let's take a look at the Fluency Pyramid and years of research.

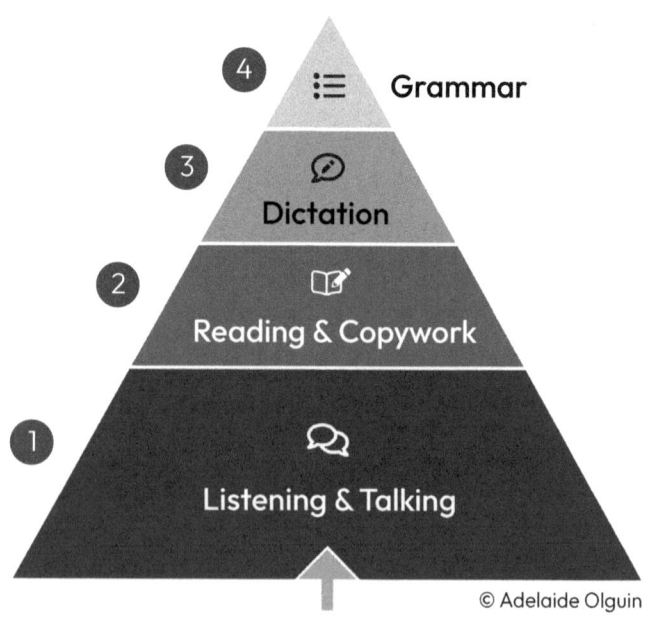

© Adelaide Olguin

**First and most important:
The foundation for fluency.**

TALKBOX.MOM

The foundation of fluency is Listening & Talking. Research shows that children need to hear over 46 million words by the age of four to prepare them for school.[9] To create a foundation for reading, a child needs to have clocked 20,000 hours of listening through infancy and early childhood. [10]

This means that just because your child can read in English, it does not mean that it's time for them to read to themselves in French. You're disregarding all the work you did as a parent in the Listening & Talking Layer for your child's first language.

What happens if you skip ahead? You slow down fluency or never reach it. For example, if your child is reading a word in French, that word should create an image or meaning in their head. The reference for this word comes from their experience of using the word in a phrase.

If your child has to translate the word from French to English, this is NOT fluency. They're translating. Therefore, you want to create a strong foundation of listening and talking before you move on to other fluency layers.

As you spend a couple of years building out the Listening and Talking layer, your child's ability to read in French will develop much faster. Then as you read and do copywork, your child's ability to do transcription will develop even faster. And if you choose next to work on formal grammar, your child will already have such a trained ear and eye for grammar that they won't lack context to quickly understand grammar principles that they already use naturally.

Notice how all the fluency layer's build on each other. This follows the natural progression found in learning a first language.

One comment that I hear as I explain fluency layers is that in English you don't know every word and you look words up in the dictionary. Exactly. You're looking up the word in English and the description in English is giving meaning to the word. A great time to start reading in French is when you can look up words in a French dictionary and understand their meaning from the description in French.

Now that you understand how important laying the foundation for the Listening & Talking Fluency Layer is... it doesn't make it any less scary! You might feel the same pull to shadow activities because they are in your comfort zone.

I would love to assign you some Fluency Layer Activities to help gently push you outside your comfort zone while you don't lose track of where your focus should be.

Fluency Layer Activities are immersion experiences that are supported by the core of the Fluency Layer. For example, the core of Listening & Talking is your Phrase Practice Sessions and using your phrases.

Some of the Fluency Layer Activities are: watching TV shows, movies, or YouTube videos, listening to music and podcasts, and, most importantly, talking to native speakers.

Do note that watching and listening to media will become shadow activities if you are not actively building out the core of Listening & Talking by practicing and using your phrases together. Likewise, you'll enjoy an accelerated progress as you talk with native speakers outside your home if you're in turn practicing and using your phrases with your family.

Here are some steps that we go into more detail in the TalkBox.Mom Signature Program that will gently help you step outside your comfort zone and grow.

First, when listening to media in French or other French speakers, listen for the words you do know. Second, feel really good about everything you DO know. Your ability to hear separate words in sentences even if you don't know what each word means is a big step.

Next, realize that it's okay not to know every word. You don't have to understand everything to get an idea of what is happening. From body language and tone, you can make educated guesses, which is what many foreigners do.

The last step can be the hardest, but, of course, it's the most important. You need to let people know that you don't understand a critical word. Ask what it means. If you can, add a note in your phone or notebook with new words or phrases you hear from other people. Most people love to help!

Likewise, if you hear a critical word repeated in any form of media you're listening to or watching in French, write that word down and then look it up later. You'll get burnt out fast if you write down everything, so really focus on words you hear repeated often.

As you step outside your comfort zone, remind yourself and your family that welcoming what you don't know instead of fearing it will help you learn faster and become more comfortable speaking French.

I've filled the next section, Your Toolbox, with phrases you can use when you are in these situations or are helping your child to say new words. I'm excited for you to slowly move outside your comfort zone— inch by inch—and look back at your progress in amazement.

Your Toolbox

♥ ☑ Got it!

♡ ☐ Say...	Dis...
♡ ☐ (to 2+)	Dites...
♡ ☐ Repeat after me...	Répète après moi...
♡ ☐ (to 2+)	Répétez après moi...
♡ ☐ How do you say...?	Comment on dit...?
♡ ☐ How do you pronounce this?	Comment ça se prononce, ça ?
♡ ☐ How do you pronounce...?	Comment on prononce...?
♡ ☐ What does this mean?	Ça veut dire quoi ça ?
♡ ☐ What does ... mean?	Ca veut dire quoi... ?
♡ ☐ Do you know what ... means?	Tu sais ce que ça veut dire... ?
♡ ☐ I don't know that word.	Je ne connais pas ce mot.
♡ ☐ Let's look it up.	Viens, on va chercher.
♡ ☐ (to 2+)	Venez, on va chercher.

♥ ☑

♡ ☐ I don't know what you said. Je n'ai pas compris ce que tu as dit.

♡ ☐ *(formal)* Je n'ai pas compris ce que vous avez dit.

♡ ☐ Would you please say it again? Tu veux bien répéter, s'il te plaît ?

♡ ☐ *(formal)* Vous voulez bien répéter, s'il vous plaît ?

♡ ☐ Would you please say it again slower? Tu veux bien répéter lentement, s'il te plaît ?

♡ ☐ *(formal)* Vous voulez bien répéter lentement, s'il vous plaît ?

♡ ☐ Please speak slower. Parle moins vite, s'il te plaît.

♡ ☐ *(formal)* Parlez moins vite, s'il vous plaît.

♡ ☐ I just started speaking French. Je commence tout juste à parler français.

♡ ☐ I learn French by talking to my kids. J'apprends le français en parlant à mes enfants.

♡ ☐ I use a system from TalkBox.Mom. J'utilise la méthode TalkBox.Mom.

Goodbye

Can we not say goodbye?

 I'd love to meet you on the blog where I share resources, inspiration, motivation, and highlight families. Comments are definitely open to chat and ask questions. www.talkbox.mom/blog

 Forget perfectly curated life and see how language learning actually looks at home and abroad. Come along with me as I help my kids speak other languages and as I help your family as well! Catch our team in our DMs. www.instagram.com/talkboxmom

 Love longer-format trainings that you can listen to as you wash dishes, fold laundry, or go on a run? Subscribe to our YouTube channel to go deeper on creating a life that lights your whole family up. www.youtube.com/talkboxmom

References

1   Mason, Charlotte M. (1925). *Home Education*, 301.
2   Mason, Charlotte M. (1925). *Home Education*, 306.
3   Mason, Charlotte M. (1925). *Home Education*, 157.
4   Mason, Charlotte M. (1925). *Home Education*, 301.
5   Mason, Charlotte M. (1925). *Home Education*, 80.
6   Mason, Charlotte M. (1925). *Home Education*, 80.
7   Mason, Charlotte M. (1925). *Home Education*, 80.
8   Mason, Charlotte M. (1925). *Home Education*, 301.
9   Hart B, Risley TR. (1999). The Social World of Children Learning to Talk.
10   Dehaene S. (2009). Reading in the Brain: The Science and Evolution of a Human Invention.

Index

A

about 154
absolutely 268
acting 140
afraid 90
again **39**, 69, 175, 259
all done **40**
all gone **41**
a lot 139
already 51, 67, 78, 162, 175, 219
always 236
another 101
answer 102
arm 140
art 202
ask 175
asleep 219
at 183
awake 97, 219

B

baby 64, 87, 97, 101, 147, 169, 176, 187, 190, 200, 207, 219, 257
baby bag **43**
baby gate **127**
babysit 45
babysitter **45**
back 140, 143, 179, 190
backpack 121, 173, 249
backyard **45**, 242
bad **47**, 221, 236, 244
ball **47**, 200, 212, 248
balloon **49**
Band-Aid **50**
baseball 225
basket **50**
basketball 225
bath **51**
bathroom 96
bathtub 62
batteries **51**
be 195
beautiful 83, 120, 151, 191, 197
because 213
bed **52**, 53, 146, 241
be missing 166

better 113
bib **55**
Bible **56**
big **56**, 177
bike 46, **56**, 179, 264
binky **57**, 108, 173
bird 157, 185
bite **58**
black 82
blanket **59**, 104, 158
bless you **59**, 222
blocks **59**
blood **61**
blow **61**, 266
blow up 49
blue 82, 218
boat **62**
boogers **62**, 63
book **63**, 105, 227
bother 227
bottle **64**, 179
bottom 264
bowl 94
box **64**, **65**, 80, 126, 179
boy 191
break 50, **65**, 83
breastfeed **66**
broccoli 134
broom **67**

TALKBOX.MOM

D

E

F

TALKBOX.MOM

night 54, 136

no **175**

noise 135, **175**

noisy 175

nose 61, 141, 143

not 223

nothing 134, 157

not yet 257

now **176**

　right now 84

nurse 66, **176**

O

ocean **177**

of course 268

off **178**, 247, 251

office 130

okay 139

old **178**, 238

older **178**

　oldest 178

on 179

one 246, 256

only 83, 91

open 65, 99, 103,
　　　127, **179**, 192,
　　　230, 247

orange 82

other 102, 252

out 43, 75

outlet 189

out of 241

outside 49, 57, 90,
　　　99, **181**, 202,
　　　226

P

pack 43, 91

page 161

pants 264

paper 82, 108, 204,
　　　235

park 130, 173, **183**

pass me 82

path **184**

pee 91, 173, 190

pet, the **184**

pet, to pet **185**

phone 121, **186**, 189

pick 63

pick up 48, 80, 154,
　　　187, 251

picture 83, 106, 119,
　　　202

piece 82, 235

pieces 126

pile 188

pillow **187**

pinch 98

pink 83

pink eye 215

pizza 163

plane 135, 248

plant 132, **188**

plate(s) 66, 78, 94,
　　　260

play 39, 45, 47, 59,
　　　69, 75, 85, 94,
　　　96, 101, 102,
　　　120, 125, 147,
　　　151, 156, 202,
　　　210, 213, 224,
　　　228, 242, 252,
　　　261, 267

play dough 162

please 198, 208, 265

plug 251

plug in **188**, 189

poke 99

poop 90, 91, **189**,
　　　221

pop 69

post office 130

potty **190**

pour 76

practice 225

praise **191**

present **192**

swing **230**

swings 184

T

table 77, 99, 157, 178, 209, **233**

tablet 189

take 47, 62, 76, 80, 164, 257

take a bath 40, 51

take a break **66**

take a picture 73

take care 97

take off 178, 205

take out 244

take turns **234**

talk **234**, 235

tall 244

tangled 133

tap 109

tape **235**

taste **236**

teacher 156

tease 228

teddy bear **236**

television 245

tell 40, 53, 223, **237**

tell me 87, 154

terrible 139

test 202

text **238**

than 201

thank you 123, 175, 263

that 258

there 157

think 44, 212

thirsty **239**

this 240, 283

three 264

through 230

throw 48, 98, 199, 244

throw away **239**

throw up 214

tie 211, **239**

time 51, 64, 77, 79, 85, 90, 103, 114, 129, 164, 171, 219, 233, **240**, 256, 265

tissue 62, **241**

to 233

today 78, 137, 189, 202, 226, 263

together 56, 63, 198, **242**

toilet 190

tomatoes 132

tomorrow 71

tonight 262

too 252

too much 129

touch 100, 189, 210

don't touch 61

tower 60

toy 50, 51, 79, 98, 102, 107, 118, 119, 158, 178, 187, 206, 207, **243**, 248

training wheels 265

trampoline 146

trash 67, 239, **244**

trash can 67, **244**

treasure 92

tree 154, 157, **244**

trip, to trip **245**

trouble 196, 203

truth 154

try 39, 190, **245**

turn, like your turn 51

turn off 101, 154, 169, 178, 246, 253

turn on 155, 169

turn up 169

TV 245, 261

Y

Z